LONG LIBERATED LADIES

MARY LEWIS COAKLEY

Long Liberated
Ladies

IGNATIUS PRESS   SAN FRANCISCO

Cover by Riz Boncan Marsella

CONTENTS

PREFACE

This book is a selective compilation of the lives of positive—sometimes powerful—women from the fourteenth century to the twentieth century.

By writing simply, yet beautifully and convincingly, about the life story of each of these outstanding women, the author, Mary Lewis Coakley, gives the reader remarkable examples of the dedicated service of women of a variety of nationalities and faiths.

Of the women who are portrayed there are queens and saints, authors and educators, powerbrokers and scientists. There are doctors of the church, founders of religious orders, warriors, pioneers, poets, and painters.

It is worthy of notice that these women of achievement preceded the feminists and their self-fulfilling demands of the 1960s and 1970s by decades and some by centuries. Each of these women looked beyond any selfish interests. Each one was, as Mrs. Coakley writes, "striving to serve a cause or a belief, or an ideal or a nation, or her fellowman, or science, and in the last analysis, consciously or unconsciously, (striving to serve) God."

Mrs. Coakley is to be commended for delving into history and bringing alive for all of us these heroic role models.

Eleanor Schlafly
President
Cardinal Mindszenty Foundation

1

ANYTHING YOU CAN DO, I CAN DO...?

WOMAN MADE AMBASSADOR TO THE POPE!
WOMAN COMMANDS IN BATTLE!
WOMAN RECEIVES SECOND NOBEL PRIZE!

Today's headlines?

No. But if in the past such events had found their way into splashy print, the first headline would have fit Catherine of Siena of the fourteenth century; the second, Joan of Arc of the fifteenth century; and the third, Marie Curie of the nineteenth century.

Still, the feminists keep telling us that women of the past were suppressed and oppressed. They say it is only since they have fought for liberation that women have dared to leave their own hearthstones and so attained any degree of success and fulfillment.

Moreover, some women in religious life and some feminist theologians complain that their predecessors were especially browbeaten, downtrodden, and put upon by male chauvinist priests and prelates. Judith Plaskow and Carol Christ declare in their book, *Woman Spirit Rising,* "Articulating and giving substance to the charge that religion is sexist has been the first job of feminist theology."

Admittedly, there are some facts to support the charges, and the feminists have told—and are still telling—the public about it in multitudinous newspaper and magazine articles, not to mention countless TV and radio programs, books, lectures, and speeches. Surely over the last couple of decades our "consciousness has been raised", so there is no use repeating any of the familiar verbiage one more time. However, there may be use in presenting the other, less-publicized side, because at long last there are signs that people will listen. After all, conditions for our foremothers were not all black. In the pre–Women's Lib era, when women had to contend with certain handicaps, they also had some compensations, some advantages that they lack today.

Even in the distant past, when churchmen, the supposed arch offenders, had a stronger voice than today and when some handicaps and hurdles indeed impeded women, they enjoyed a few important advantages that they have now lost—and, moreover, have now lost sight of.

To begin with, in the days when churchmen were dominant and were heeded more than they are today, they constantly lauded Mary, Jesus' Mother. Indirectly, their praise of Mary helped all women. Churchmen taught that Mary, the Queen of saints, was the prime exemplar. She occupied a higher niche than any other nondivine person. In every cathedral, basilica, church, or wayside chapel, they set up a statue or a picture of her, and they hailed her as the human figure above all (except the God-man) who had ever trod, or will ever tread, this lowly planet Earth.

Now, Mary did what obviously no man can or could do; she bore within her body and nourished with her own blood and fed at her breasts the one human being who was also divine, the Being who is one in substance with the Father, the *Ens Necessarium* who created, sustains, and rules all creation.

Granted, those churchmen of yore, as those of today, affixed a "No Admittance" sign on the door to the priesthood; still, this was more than offset by the Marian homage. After all, most men in those days, unlike most men in our day, firmly believed Christ was God, the second Person of the Blessed Trinity, so they were awed by the female creature who was his Mother, and they reasoned, at least subconsciously, that if one woman is so exalted, it followed that all women are somewhat exalted through her; Mary's status lends honor to her sex.

So because of Mary, men showed a shade more reverential courtesy and respectful deference to all women than they did to men. There was a long period—in fact it lasted into the beginning of our century—when chivalry was a reality. Although most feminists today scoff at chivalry, they can hardly know what they are scoffing at. Today's feminist leaders, as well as women of the immediate past, did their best to destroy the surviving remnants of chivalry so that the present generation has never experienced it.

Besides chivalry, our foremothers enjoyed other advantages. In the far past, in the so-called Ages of Faith, even the worldly and the wicked were a bit in awe of sanctity. But sanctity, as St. Paul said, is "neither male nor female. For you are all one in Christ Jesus" (Gal 3:28). In other words, women have the same opportunities to attain sanctity as do men.

Indeed, they seem to have an edge, for women appear to be endowed with a congenital bent toward piety and holiness that men lack, and in times past men conceded this. The Little Office of the Blessed Virgin, which literally millions of monks, nuns, and even some laymen have said through the ages, prays for "the devout female sex".

Even closer to our own time we see that until recent years, men have often reverenced women for their supposed goodness and holiness. When a colleague asked Louis Pasteur why he, a brilliant scientist with a vast fund of knowledge, was a fervent believer, indeed "as fervent a believer as a Breton peasant", the great scientist answered, "It is precisely because I do know a great deal that I am as devout as a Breton peasant man. But if I knew more, I would be as devout as a Breton peasant *woman.*"

A modern pope remarked on women's bent toward sanctity. In his book *Illustrissimi,* John Paul I (Albino Luciano) declared, "Woman is more sensitive to religion. . . . Hence the vast host of woman saints, mystics." And he spoke of the "women who started ascetic-theological movements with wide-ranging influence", citing Marcella, who helped St. Jerome translate the Bible; Madame Acarie, who influenced "the entire French spirituality of the early seventeenth century"; the German princess Amalia von Gallitzin, a spiritual force in her native land; and Russian convert Sophie Swetchine of the early nineteenth century, who lived in France and was "the spiritual guide of the most outstanding laymen and priests".

Admittedly, some of these women are unfamiliar to us Americans, but we do know that the first U.S. citizen the Catholic Church canonized was a woman, Frances Cabrini; the first native-born American citizen that it canonized was also a woman, Elizabeth Bayley Seton.

Obviously, no saintly person could be so prideful as to seek worldly honors; if she did, she would cease to be saintly. However, by a strange paradox, saintliness in the past often brought not only canonization after death, but in some cases it brought honors and recognition during a person's lifetime. The fourteenth-century pope in Avignon, having turned a deaf ear to kings and cardinals, would not have listened to Catherine of Siena either, much less followed her counsel, had he not believed her holy. The French dauphin would not have made Joan of Arc his *chef de guerre* if he had not felt that she was heaven inspired, nor would the men have accepted as leader this "wench of low degree", as one knight called her, if they had not believed the same.

Then women directing convents and monasteries, be they

holy or not quite so holy, were in ages past looked up to and, in some instances, were as influential as any courtier or king. The nun Mary Agreda served as counselor, or unofficial secretary of state, to King Philip IV of Spain. Had she not been an abbess, Philip would not have noticed her. As it was, he came to rely on her advice. When he could not go to see her, he wrote her question-filled letters. He would write on only one side of the paper, and she would write her answers on the blank side.

These letters were later printed in book form, and they, as well as Mary Agreda's book *The Mystical City of God,* are still in print and have been translated into many languages.

Now another advantage for women of the past is that when most nations were kingdoms and when the throne was hereditary and carried with it much power, women headed nations more often than they do today, despite the Corazon Aquinos and the Margaret Thatchers. In the thirteenth century when Louis VIII of France, the husband of Blanche of Castile, died, the heir, her son Louis IX, was only eleven years old, so Queen Blanche became regent and ruled France in his stead. Capable, though definitely authoritarian, she first governed for eight years, the equivalent of two terms of our presidency; then some years later when Louis IX went off to the Crusades, Blanche was again regent, this time for six years. But to say that she ruled France for a total of fourteen years is somewhat of an understatement. All the while Louis IX sat on the throne, Blanche (according to historian Hilaire Belloc) breathed down her son's neck and guided practically every move he made. Need we remind ourselves that we moderns in the United States, despite our Women's Movement and our National Organization of Women (NOW), have not as yet elected a woman as chief executive?

Nor were our foremothers shut out of the business world. In his book *The World's First Love,* Bishop Fulton J. Sheen said that "up to the seventeenth century in England, women engaged in business and perhaps even more so than today . . . so many wives were in business that it was provided by law that the husbands should not be responsible for their debts."

But leaving far-off times and moving closer to our own day, though still the pre–Women's Lib era, we see that women were honored in our grandmothers' time in ways that they are seldom honored today.

True, fewer outside jobs were easily accessible to those women than to us, but on the other hand, our grandmothers would not have been shamefaced because they did not have an outside job. Scarcely a one of them would have called herself a "mere housewife", because the housewife role was universally considered normal and hence quite honorable. Because it was harder to obtain certain jobs, most of our grandmothers would have thought (wrongly perhaps) that they could not become lawyers, bankers, financiers, doctors, and so on, although some women in those days did pursue such careers.

Here in these United States of America, there was Elizabeth Blackwell (1821–1910), who in 1857 founded and managed, with other women doctors, a hospital in New York City. There was Clara Barton (1821–1912), whom President Lincoln appointed to search for missing soldiers during the Civil War and who later established the American Red Cross. There was Dorothea Dix (1802–87), who pioneered in bringing specialized treatment to the insane (until she appeared on the scene, the insane were often imprisoned with criminals) and who served as supervisor of women's nurses during the Civil War. There was Belva Lockwood (1830–1917), a lawyer who tried cases before the United States Supreme Court in 1870. There was Julia Ward Howe (1819–1910), lecturer, newspaper editor, and writer, who produced the masterpiece the "Battle Hymn of the Republic". There was Helen Hunt Jackson (1831–85), a sociologist whom the U.S. government commissioned to look into the conditions of the Indians in California, who is better remembered today for her novel *Ramona*.

Indeed, there are countless others, among them Hetty Green, the Wall Street wizard; Margaret Haughterty, the intrepid entrepreneur and philanthropist of New Orleans to whom the city raised a statue; Mary Lyon, who founded Mt. Holyoke College and who was elected to the American Hall of Fame; and Martha McChesney Berry, who established schools for poor whites and Negroes in her native Georgia and to whom President Theodore Roosevelt awarded a medal for outstanding service to the nation.

Why go on? Granted these women were exceptions in the nineteenth century, still, be it repeated, the women who did remain housebound housewives were more often than today considered to have a highly honorable profession. Hence they did not have to apologize for their role nor marshal arguments to justify it. The arguments, however, were, and are, there.

First of all, a "homebody" is not necessarily a nobody. She might be a mother, and a mother is usually the person who sees the most of a child in his early years; obviously, then, she has the greatest influence on his character. Now, what's more important: to rear (as many a mother does) a person of upright character or to erect (as many an engineer does) a bridge spanning a river?

Businessmen may be concerned with coworker relations, labor relations, public relations, and employee relations, but always the relationship is with those whose characters are formed. Not so mothers. They have an opportunity to mold unformed characters mentally and spiritually; hence, mothers rank among the most important of mortals. They

can predispose a human being to become a saint or a
scoundrel, an industrialist or an idler, a reasonably well-
informed citizen or an ignoramus.

In fact, according to some psychiatrists and psychologists,
mothers can greatly influence the mental health of their
children. The *Wall Street Journal* (Mar. 3, 1987) carried an
article saying that certain psychologists believe that a
mother just by keeping her child (especially during his first,
most formative eighteen months of life) at home in an
unchanging environment and close to herself, gives him a
sense of security and a better chance of mental stability than
does the mother who puts him into a day-care center so
many hours per week.

Yes, "the hand that rocks the cradle, rules the world."

But what of childless housewives? They are VIPs too, and
those of the pre–Women's Lib era recognized this. Certainly
they didn't feel demeaned by the "housewife" tag as do so
many moderns. Although they might have agreed with the
moderns that some household tasks are boring or grubby,
they would not have denied, as do the feminists, that many
other household jobs are a mental challenge. Women of our
grandmothers' day realized that to handle these tasks, a
housewife must develop varied skills, so perhaps she has a
broader life than her career-oriented sister. On a small scale,
a housewife in many cases had to be an interior decorator,
a cook, a seamstress, a chauffeur, a gardener, a caterer, an
economist, a dietitian, a purchasing agent, a maintenance
person, a bookkeeper, a cashier, a hostess, a social secretary,
an efficiency expert—the list could go on and on.

But despite these multiple jobs, the old-time housebound
housewife is freer than is the woman who works outside
the home. The latter must please her boss, or the board of
directors, or her customers, or her clients, or her patients.
The former is her own boss. She may work on the double

one day and slow down on the next. She sets her own work schedule; she may make the beds at 7 A.M. or at 2 P.M. She may fashion her own clothes, or she may buy them at a convenient boutique. She may knit sweaters, or she may never pick up a ball of yarn. She may raise vegetables in the backyard, or she may defrost cellophane-wrapped frozen vegetables. She may make chocolate cake, or she may find a handy bakery.

Then she has no time clock to punch, no train or bus to catch, no rush-hour traffic to fight driving to and from work, no "appointed rounds" to make every morning and evening whether it is raining, snowing, or sleeting. Moreover, once the children are in school—if she has children—she can, unless she's incredibly inefficient, find for herself the luxury of a few extra and odd moments in the day. These lagniappes she may spend as she wishes; she may indulge in an afternoon nap, or drop in on a neighbor, or play tennis, or manage some volunteer work, or scribble poetry, or breed dogs, or read history, or study Greek, or take up painting, or . . . or . . . or . . . Perhaps her housewife job (especially the modern housewife job, with mechanized conveniences) is the only one in the whole wide world that allows such flexibility.

But the housewife job is far more than a job; it is essentially a vocation, or at least the "wife" part is. By nature, the wife, rather than the husband, is usually the morale booster and the creator and upholder of emotional stability in a marriage. Or, to use the oft-repeated phrase, "If the man is the head of the home, the woman is its very heart."

To be a good wife with even the best of husbands requires intuition and intelligence, tact and tenderness. The woman who does not have to struggle with the demands of an outside career (which may involve traveling and absences from home for days on end, or occasional late hours at the office, or evening calls on clients, and the like) may devote more time, thought, and energy to the basic role of a wife and so be more successful at it. Present-day divorce rates indicate as much. Another *Wall Street Journal* article (Dec. 9, 1986) cited separate surveys of men and of women corporate officers. Women officers had divorce rates five times those of men officers.

In his book *Men and Marriage,* George Gilder cited facts and figures to prove that single men are "five times more likely to commit violent crime than married men". He also noted that "single men have almost double the mortality rate of married men", and he concluded that when a man in "accepting an honor . . . gives credit to his wife, he is not merely following a ritual. He is stating a practical fact. In all likelihood he would not have succeeded if he had been single or divorced."

So success in the role of wife is not trivial. Certainly it can be argued that for a wife to make one man's life happy, smooth, and contented as well as inspire him to develop his potential over many years requires as much skill as for a woman lawyer to win numerous divorce cases for her clients over a span of many years. Certainly, too, the "devoted wife" role is not an inferior role, since as George Gilder pointed out, it usually means that the wife rather than the husband is the bulwark of the marriage and hence the bulwark of society.

Women of the past knew this, and it gave them assurance. They also had the assurance, which women of today lack, that their marriage was generally assumed to be permanent. Today, with our sexual revolution so championed by the feminists, the marriage vow is considered less binding. This means, in practice, that couples may part with comparative ease, and this often creates worse problems for the woman than for the man. She may have to rear the children alone and also support them on less material means than she would have had in marriage.

Then acceptance of abortion, again so promoted by the feminists as emancipation from "the slavery of reproduction", doesn't actually help women. On the contrary! If an unmarried woman becomes pregnant, her sex partner may tell her, "Here's money for an abortion", or he may walk away without a word. In times past, and in the memory of many of us, the man in most cases would have felt some obligation to marry the woman he had impregnated or at least to contribute to the child's support.

Still, all of this is not to say that succeeding in business, or in politics, or in any public career is to be disdained. Anyone can understand why a woman would be gratified to have a high-paying, prestigious job; anyone can understand why she is anxious to use all her talents, including those of value in the marketplace; anyone can understand that a woman is reluctant to give up or postpone an outside career if and when she assumes the wife-mother role. Quite naturally, she would like to have both an outside career and parenthood (as does a man), even though for her (and not for him) the dual role requires great juggling skill and creates a certain tension. All that has been said so far is that women of the past, though they were less often allowed to attempt the juggling act, had some compensations for the restraints, so their "oppression" and "suppression" are in part, at least, a figment of the feminists' imagination.

The rest of the book will show through biographical sketches what some talented women—women who were not exposed to the feminist virus that began spreading back in the 1960s—have done in the past. The account will begin with women of the far past, then go on to women of the more recent past. It will not include women of the immediate past, such as Kate Smith, Corrie ten Boom, and

Ethel Waters, nor women who, though still alive, owe nothing to the Women's Movement. (Women in the last category are amazingly numerous. Jeane Kirkpatrick, Margaret Thatcher, Clare Boothe Luce, Chiara Lubich, Helen Hayes, Phyllis Schlafly, Mother Teresa of Calcutta, and Mother Angelica of TV fame leap to the mind. They deserve a separate book.)

Despite handicaps and restraints, these long liberated ladies of the past included here managed to have brilliant careers.

How did these women do it? What special quality did these women have that perhaps modern feminists lack?

That question is not easy to answer in a word, but after reading the biographies, the answer to the question should be as clear as the handwriting that Baltasar saw on the wall. And it may convince us that "Anything they can do we can do" not necessarily better, or even as well, but do to some extent—can we not? And we can do it without adopting the feminists' philosophy—can we not?

2

DIPLOMAT EXTRAORDINAIRE

Catherine of Siena
(1347–1380)

Where kings and cardinals failed, Catherine succeeded.

She was persistent, persuasive, and powerful. One writer, James Walsh, called her "the most important woman . . . and very probably the most important personage in the Europe of her day."

When she was only a young girl, she was sent by certain Italian city-states to treat with potentates and princes and to arrange peace in troubled and ticklish situations. She served in this capacity so often that one might say she practiced "shuttle diplomacy".

On the surface, her background did not seem to fit her for a diplomatic career. Her parents were middle-grounders in every sense, neither aristocrats nor lowly serfs, neither intellectuals nor ignoramuses, neither wealthy nor wanting in this world's goods. Catherine's father, Giacomo di Benincasa, made a comfortable enough living as a dyer of wool, and neither he nor Catherine's mother, Lapa (the daughter of a local poet), nor Catherine's many siblings did anything unusual or spectacular. Naturally everybody expected Catherine when she grew up to adopt the pattern set by her older sisters and of most of the other women in her hometown Siena. This meant becoming betrothed in her teens, marrying soon after, setting up her own household, and rearing a family.

But Catherine did not fit the mold. First of all, as a child she was more precocious and more pious than the average. When she was a very small dimpled darling, perhaps it was amusing that she was always praying, but as she grew a little older this piety became annoying, especially since she added penances to the prayers. Then her parents were jolted when she joined the Mantellate, a group of religious women who, though not nuns, were affiliated with the Dominican Order. (They still exist today, and are called the Third Order Dominicans.)

"Well, at least this doesn't stop Catherine from marrying," Lapa philosophized, "and the sooner the better, before she gets any more crazy ideas." And as a prudent parent, she forthwith made betrothal arrangements for Catherine.

When the girl, now fifteen years old, was told about this, she answered with a shocker, "When I was only seven years old, I made a vow of virginity."

What? The stunned Lapa was speechless for a full minute before she began to harangue Catherine and mutter about getting a dispensation. But Catherine did not want a dispensation, and to prove she meant to forego marriage, she "disfigured herself" (so Lapa ranted) and reduced her marriage desirability by cutting off her long, chestnut-colored hair.

"All right, my girl," said Lapa in effect, "If you want to be a spinster, I'll dismiss my kitchen maid and you can do her work. We'll see how you like that!"

Catherine seemed to like it quite well. At any rate, she washed the pots and pans and roasted the meat with a song or a prayer, and she found time too to think long thoughts, to attend Mass, and to visit the townspeople when she could help them.

Soon Catherine's father was won over, and he asked Lapa as well as his children to leave the girl alone. Moreover, he reminded them that by dedicating her virginity to God, Catherine was becoming, in the popular phrase, "a bride of Christ", and he said, "We could never have obtained so honorable a marriage for her; instead of mortal man we have been given the immortal, God-made man."

By now Catherine felt ready to begin her life's work. She wanted to dedicate her life to God through serving his "least brethen", and she knew no better way to begin than by working in the local hospital, Santa Maria della Scala. She took care of cancerous patients that other attendants shied away from, and she soon won a reputation not only for skill but for selflessness. When the plague ravaged Siena, she worked with the ill and the dying to the point of heroism. The whole town admired her and sang her praises.

They also liked her. Apparently she had great charisma, and people, ill or well, flocked to her, so that by the time she was sixteen, she had a following, a group of disciples of both sexes, who called themselves the "Caterinati". This group grew and grew in size, and Catherine found herself the rage of Siena.

It's a temptation to say that the Caterinati looked to Catherine as people today look at Anne Landers for advice about their personal lives. It's also a temptation to say that some of them looked to her as poets and novelists looked to Madame de Staël, for many of the literati were among the Caterinati. Both statements, however, are inadequate and trivial, because Catherine's advice had a spiritual depth that neither Landers nor de Staël would or could lay claim to. (Catherine was an extraordinary soul who later experienced mystical death; while her body seemed lifeless, she was caught up into ecstatic union with God. Later too, she bore in her hands and her feet invisible stigmata.)

Catherine's advice was not always spoken; some of it was written, and she kept several of the Caterinati busy acting

as her secretaries, turning out letters by the dozen. Her
secretaries avowed that she would dictate letters to several
of them at once, without confusion.

She wrote not only to friends, acquaintances, and fellow
countrymen, but she also wrote to churchmen and politicians when she wanted to commend or to question their
policies. These letters had a faint resemblance to letters that
a concerned citizen of the United States might write to his
congressman; however, the recipients, finding her observa-
tions astute, responded not with form letters but with letters
asking advice.

It was not very long before papal legates actually consulted
this unusual young girl about Church affairs, and her own
townspeople as well as ecclesiastics employed her as a
negotiator when factions threatened civil war.

There was often a dispute or feud going on. Dante wrote
in disgust, "The laws of the Sienese made in October aren't
valid in November", because if one faction was in power,
it would overturn the law of the preceding faction as well
as try to punish the vanquished.

Indeed there was much conflict throughout Italy and in
all of Europe. The Holy Roman Empire and the papacy were
locked in a power struggle, and, consequently, so were the
two political parties of the era, the Ghibellines, who
supported the Empire, and the Guelphs, who supported the
papacy. To gain a power advantage, each side sometimes
purposely stirred up conflict.

In Italy opposition to the papacy was based on understandable resentment that a succession of seven popes—all
Frenchmen—had lived and were living, not in the traditional Church center of Rome, but in Avignon, France,
where they often kowtowed to the French king. Franciscan
monks coined the derisive epithet "Babylonian captivity"
for this situation.

Although most of the French popes were good men, they must have been myopic, for they added insult to injury by appointing their fellow countrymen, not Italians, as legates and governors of Church-owned provinces in Italy. Dante taunted that the Pope had married the papacy to France and that he was no more than a lowly chaplain for the French king.

Petty princes and feudal lords throughout Italy took advantage of the situation. Knowing that the people, in their resentment of the absent, pro-French Pope, would raise no objection, they seized bits and pieces here and there of papal territory.

Pope Innocent VI, who reigned when Catherine was a child, tried to right some of the mistakes of his predecessors, but since he continued to stay in Avignon (despite pleas from another liberated lady, Bridget of Sweden), he could not placate powerful men like the duke of Milan, who welcomed an excuse to augment their power and possessions. The duke spurned all papal overtures and moves toward peace and continued to seize and annex papal territory in Italy where, tyrant that he was, he oppressed his tenants abominably. The Pope countered by sending him a bull of excommunication, which further enraged the fiery duke. He forced the messenger to swallow not only the parchment on which the bull was written, but its seal and its silken cords too. Then he turned the air blue with swearing and declarations that he, the duke, was pope, emperor, and God on his own land.

When Innocent VI died, Urban V, a truly holy man, succeeded him, and the "Peace of Milan" was effected, but it was short lived. By the time that Catherine entered the scene as a factor, enmity between the Guelphs and the Ghibellines was as fierce as, if not fiercer than, ever.

It is amazing that in her many diplomatic missions, Catherine persuaded so many cities to sheath their swords and make peace with the Pope. The Pope sent her to the towns of Lucca and Pisa to secure their neutrality. (It was in Pisa that she received the invisible stigmata.) But a more important mission was to Florence.

The city magistrates of Florence met her with great pomp at the gates of the town. Once her mission was accomplished there, the magistrates proposed that she go on a mission to the Pope in Avignon and persuade him to lift the interdict he had imposed on the city. They promised that their ambassadors would follow her and endorse any settlement she could work out. The terms were up to her; they said they would trust her judgment. So Catherine set out for France to see the then-reigning Gregory XI.

He was not a bad sort, but on the other hand he was not remarkably good or strong either. He owed his start up the ecclesiastical ladder to nepotism. While he was a boy in his early teens, his uncle, Pope Clement VI, gave Gregory several benefices, and when he was eighteen, made him a cardinal. He then studied canon law and theology at the University of Perugia and became a widely recognized expert in these subjects. This qualified him, twenty-two years later (two popes having reigned since his uncle's death) to be elected Pope, although during all the years that he had been a cardinal, he had never been ordained a priest. A few days after the papal election, he saw to it that ordination took place.

When Catherine spoke to him in her persuasive way as a Florentine delegate, he agreed to most of her terms. Still, Catherine's mission was not successful because the Florentines did not fulfill their promise of sending ambassadors to sign the pact she had made. In effect, they played her false, and they did not trust her after all.

Although Catherine sent the Florentines a strongly worded letter denouncing them for failure to do their part, she promptly turned her attention to a matter that was uppermost in her mind. She was concerned about reform of the clergy and return of the Pope to Rome. She used this face-to-face meeting with the Pope to urge an end to the Babylonian captivity. Historian John Farrow said, "Boldly, she told Gregory his errors and his weaknesses and . . . she stressed the fact that his presence in Rome was a dire necessity."

His attendants, both lay and clerical, were appalled by what they considered her effrontery. But the calm Catherine, without twitching an eyebrow, went on urging and pleading in an even and ever-respectful tone, while the Pope sat there and listened like a child chided by his mother.

Was this because the Pope felt guilty? Was it because he was weak and incapable of defending himself?

These things may have had something to do with it, but the main reason was that the Pope respected and admired Catherine's reputation for sanctity. He was convinced that this holy girl was pleading not for a personal favor but for what she sincerely believed to be the good of Christ's Church.

Some of the cardinals were less impressed; they were almost ready to remove Catherine bodily, and three theologians did step forward to ask why she, not a man, and not a clergyman, was on such a mission. Then they took her aside, and for the rest of the day from early afternoon until nightfall, they plied her with abstruse theological questions. To their amazement, she answered all the questions as though she were more learned than they. They must have felt almost as confounded as the elders in the temple when the twelve-year-old Jesus answered questions so expertly, because after all (as Catherine would have said), it was he who spoke through her.

In the end, the cardinals admitted to the Pope, "She knows

whereof she speaks." Indeed one of them said she had a clearer insight into spiritual matters than anyone he had ever encountered.

Catherine went back to her pleading with the Pope. He listened calmly until she startled him by asking, "Haven't you bound yourself by vow to return to Rome?"

Gregory turned ashen, and his hands began to shake. He had made a vow before his election to the papacy that if he were ever pope, he would go back to the Eternal City. But he had told nobody. How did Catherine know of it?

Today some people would say she had ESP or that she made a lucky surmise, but the Pope thought she must have a heavenly revelation. He was almost on the point of promising to go to Rome when a servant delivered a letter from a French cardinal; the letter warned him that if he went, the Italians, who resented his French nationality and his French sympathies, would poison him.

He showed Catherine the letter, and she answered, "Your Holiness, there is no less poison in Avignon than in Italy, and if I can travel to Avignon from Italy, so can your enemies."

Still, Catherine had to leave France without the Pope's definite promise. She may have thought she failed, but her words stuck in the Pope's mind like an irritating burr, and finally he acted: he set sail from Marseilles for Italy.

Landing in Genoa, he found (by Divine Providence, Catherine would have said) that she happened to be in that city. She had gone east by a slower overland route, and once she reached Genoa, the illness of her secretary kept her there for weeks.

When Gregory heard that she was in town, he went to see her, unannounced and dressed in the simple cassock of an ordinary priest. Catherine instantly did him homage as supreme pontiff. Though he had traveled as far as Genoa, he told her his cardinals were strongly urging him to turn back to Avignon, because the news that greeted him on disembarking was that the Florentines had soundly defeated his army and that feeling against him was running higher than ever. Who could guarantee that an assassin would not reach him and, with one lunge of a dagger, do away with him? Retreat was only common sense.

Catherine had to begin pleading all over again. She must have been eloquent, because her words were more effective than the words of several cardinals. Gregory took the road to Rome. Shortly afterward he entered the Eternal City seated on a white mule and received a tumultuous welcome.

Thus ended the Babylonian captivity, which had lasted nearly three-quarters of a century. Catherine was victor! As one biographer said, "She was the woman who swayed the destinies of Europe and of the Church."

But she did not bask in glory. She returned to Siena, where for the next year or so, she led a comparatively quiet life being a good neighbor and lending a helping hand to all around her.

Her retirement ended when the Pope sent her on a peace mission to Florence. It was a highly dangerous mission, for the city was a seething cauldron. The Pope's presence in Italy had not brought instant law and order. Those who had seized papal property were not glad to see the Pope return nor were the outlaws, who felt they had a freer hand in his absence. Homes of leading citizens were often attacked and plundered by unruly mobs or, in some instances, burned to the ground. Those courageous souls who tried to put a stop to the unruliness and who counseled peace were literally driven out of town under threat of death.

Catherine was staying at a large home atop a hill on the west bank of the Arno. One night, the eerie light of fires showed that a horde of ruffians was streaming across the

Ponte Vecchio toward the house. A cry went up, "We'll get the Sienese witch. We'll tear her to pieces."

Catherine, who was in the garden at the time, heard it, and then presto the mob was swarming over the garden wall and through its gate yelling, "Where is the accursed woman?"

The girl faced them and said simply, "I am Catherine." Then she knelt and began to pray.

Her calmness disconcerted the ruffians. They stood there dumbly a moment, then turned tail and slunk away.

Still, the wise course seemed to be for Catherine to move out and go into hiding.

Her peace efforts helped, but peace was rather long in coming. When Catherine returned to Siena for another comparatively quiet period, she used her time to write her *Dialogues,* or *Treatise on Divine Providence.* Some critics have compared her fine writing to that of Dante and Petrarch. Today the *Dialogues* and 400 of her letters are still extant. There are 150 letters to popes, cardinals, and bishops and 130 letters to kings and princes.

When Gregory died, immediately the "Western Schism" or the "Great Schism" split the Church into rival sectors. The Italians said, "No more French popes. Only an Italian will do." The French cardinals insisted, "We need a Frenchman."

The College of Cardinal Electors started to assemble, and when sixteen prelates had gathered together awaiting more to come, the Roman populace took matters into its own hands. It firmly shut and bolted the gates of the city to debar more French cardinals. Then a mob, of drunken, noisy riff-raff, thronged around the building where the election was to take place, raucously shouting, "Give us an Italian pope!"

Although additional Frenchmen were debarred, the French cardinals present still outnumbered the Italian. Happily, the

French were prudent enough to elect, nonetheless, an Italian, Bartolomeo Prignano, archbishop of Bari, who took the name Urban.

The news was announced to the mob, but in the hubbub, the word *Bari* was misunderstood; the mob thought that a French prelate had been elected. The resulting uproar was such that the cardinals feared for their lives.

To calm the mob, someone grabbed an elderly Italian cardinal, threw a papal robe over his shoulders, and shoved him onto the low balcony where the crowd could see his familiar Roman face.

Instantly the mob surged forward trying to get to the bogus pope to do him reverence. His stammered denials and explanations went unheard, so for months afterward confusion reigned. Many people throughout Christendom, receiving different reports from Rome, did not know who was the duly elected pontiff, and the opponents of Urban VI stirred up trouble, continuing to press the claims of the other man.

As though this were not enough, a group of French cardinals illegitimately elected a Frenchman, who took the name Clement VII, and France, Spain, Scotland, and Naples recognized him, while England, Flanders, Hungary, and most of northern Italy recognized Urban VI.

Catherine supported the legitimately elected Urban and urged others to do so by writing innumerable letters to princes and influential personages in Europe.

She also wrote Urban respectfully urging him to be patient and to keep his naturally harsh and hasty temper under control, for many well-meaning people were truly confused as to who was the legitimate pope.

Far from resenting her advice, the Pope paid her the unprecedented compliment of summoning her to Rome so that he might have her closer as a counselor. After she arrived there in the fall of 1378, she wrote, if possible, more letters than ever.

But letter writing was not her only service for Urban. She begged God to let her bear in her body the punishment of the sin that may have caused the distressing papal crisis, and she prayed unceasingly for the unity and the reformation of the Church.

She became ill, and after three months of extreme suffering, she died. Her last political feat was the reconciliation of Urban with the Roman republic that had supported his opponent. Then in fairly short order, most of Christendom acknowledged Urban.

Catherine was only thirty-three when she died, yet in her short life, she accomplished more than the vast majority of modern women who live into old age. How? How did she do it? The liberated lady and Nobel Prize winner Sigrid Undset said in her biography of Catherine that she "who handled powerful men so masterfully, who had such an unusual understanding of character, . . . who succeeded in making peace, . . . who prevented war . . . she would answer her contemporaries in her letters and conversations and in the *Dialogues* that . . . Christ was the only source of her courage and strength and wisdom."

3

HEROINE WITH A HALO

Joan of Arc

(1412–1431)

Saint or witch? Mere mascot or general of genius? Selfless maid of Orleans or self-seeking, prematurely born feminist, avid for power and notoriety? Whatever opinion one holds, everyone agrees that Joan of Arc was like a meteor flashing across the sky. Her life, though short, was brilliant and dramatic, and it changed the course of history.

Probably the reason she has both bitter enemies and fiercely devoted supporters is because she was such a positive person that no one who knows her story can be indifferent to her.

One modern biographer called her "arrogant and infuriating" and questioned her veracity. Another praised her as "a woman ahead of her times". The English poet Lord Byron called her "a fanatical strumpet", while the French novelist Anatole France was patronizing. The American humorist and storyteller Mark Twain rhapsodized that hers was "the most notable life ever born into this world, save only One." The English essayist and detective story writer Gilbert Keith Chesterton was almost as laudatory; he called her "a star, a thunderbolt, a diamond among pebbles, the one white stone of history". The Irish-born dramatist and satirist George Bernard Shaw tremendously admired what he called her "genius", but about the rest he took a facetious tone, joking that she was "the pioneer for sensible clothes for women". The Pope had the last word; he canonized her.

Her life is open for all to see. It is probably the best-documented life in history, because when she was on trial, her vengeful judges, hoping to uncover dark secrets, insisted that every detail of her past be dug up and exposed to their prying eyes. We know what she ate, drank, and wore on many occasions, as well as what she did and what she said.

She was born in a small French village of hard-working peasant parents. The time was the early fifteenth century when the Hundred Years War between England and France had been raging for nearly a full century. Joan's family was at the edge of that war. Except when raids, looting, and other horrors of the conflict came close, the family led a quiet life. Joan's father and brothers tilled the land from sunup to sundown, while she learned from her mother the art of the needle and the spindle.

As a child, she played with the other village children beneath a big beech tree atop a knoll overlooking the river Meuse. With them, she sang, danced, and sometimes pretended that fairies sang and danced there too. Joan also remembered that God and his holy people in heaven, though invisible, were truly with her; definitely they were not pretend people.

When Joan was twelve years old, a marvel suddenly burst like a rocket on her horizon. She saw, or thought she saw, the Archangel Michael, St. Catherine, and St. Margaret and heard them speak. They made startling statements. They told her that she was to drive the English back to their island and that she was also to defeat the allies of the English, the Burgundians. Finally, she was to arrange for the rightful heir of France, the dauphin, to be crowned as King Charles VII.

Down-to-earth personality that she was, Joan saw no way to perform these feats, and she said so. Her visitors answered that she would find a way, for the Lord would help her.

Did she still doubt? And did she doubt the vision and voices themselves? At any rate, she told absolutely no one—not her mother, her father, or her brothers—about her visitors.

They continued to come again and again. Sometimes she heard only their voices, at other times she saw their forms too. They spoke of her future mission, and gradually they became more specific about ways and means. When she was seventeen, they told her to visit a cousin of hers and his wife in a nearby town. Without telling her parents the real reason for going, she set out.

Her cousin, then, was the first person she told about the visitors. His initial reaction was, "That's crazy!" She was not surprised; it had taken her five years to muster courage to speak, but now she spoke at length, and her sincerity convinced her cousin that she was telling exactly what had happened. He wanted to help her, so he introduced her to a minor official named de Beaudricourt, who might be able to lead her to the dauphin.

De Beaudricourt scoffed at Joan's "foolishness", and he made coarse remarks about her personally, joking, "I'll turn you over to the pleasure of my soldiers." No, he emphatically did not believe she had a heaven-inspired mission to save France!

Joan ignored his rudeness and vulgarity and argued her case. What is more, she returned to see him and argued her case further. Then in time, amazingly, he admitted, at least grudgingly, that he could not dismiss this transparently sincere girl as a fraud. Nor could he believe her a deluded neurotic, for so much of what she said about everything else was such clear common sense that it seemed brilliance.

De Beaudricourt ended by entrusting her to two idealistic and eager young knights who believed they would serve *la belle France* as well as *le bon Dieu* by helping "the Maid". They obtained a horse for her. Then they swore "on their sacred honor" to escort her with all respect and chastity on an eleven-day gallop across France that would bring her to the dauphin in Chinon castle. Their only question was, "Mademoiselle, when do you want to set out?"

Joan answered, "Today rather than tomorrow. Tomorrow rather than the day after."

They traveled at night, and they sheathed their horses' iron shoes to muffle the sound of hoof beats as they crossed enemy territory. By day they hid and tried to get some sleep lying on the bare ground or on the stone or dirt floors of abandoned or burned-out houses that the English had left in their wake. Worse than the constant fear of capture by the English was the bitter cold. It was February—a particularly wet February in which icy rain seemed to fall almost unceasingly.

Surely Joan said *"Deo gratias"* when the gray battlements of Chinon castle loomed up. One of the knights delivered to the dauphin within Joan's message requesting an audience.

Since de Beaudricourt had sent word ahead to the dauphin and had also talked to friends about this "strange Maid", rumors had reached Charles' ears before she arrived. He was curious to see her, as he might have been to see a dancing bear or a deft juggler. He sent her word that he would receive her, and to add to the fun, he devised a little game. He held a huge formal reception for her with 300 courtiers attending, but he did not seat himself on his throne in princely robes to preside over the assembly. Instead, he mingled with the crowd, thinking that Joan would then be unable to recognize him.

He smiled as he waited for her to come, imagining how flustered she would be. He thought too that she would be so dazzled by the many flambeaux in the *grande salle* and by the courtiers' brilliant dress that she would be dumbfounded and unable even to ask, "Which one is the dauphin?"

Nothing worked as planned. Joan entered the *grande salle*.

Her eyes swept its seventy-foot length. Then she made her way through the crowd directly to him. She did him homage as though she were quite used to court etiquette and without preliminaries declared, "Illustrious Lord Dauphin, I, the Maid, have been sent by God to give succor to the kingdom and to you."

"But I am not the dauphin", Charles answered.

Joan looked him in the eye, and courteously but firmly dared to contradict him, "In God's name, gentle sire, you are."

Charles gasped almost audibly. How could she be so sure? He led her aside to question her privately, but she seized the initiative and told him secret thoughts and fears that he had never divulged to anyone, not even his confessor. Now Charles was actually agape. This was no ordinary maiden!

Still, in the days ahead he, shilly-shallying creature that he was, could not bring himself to supply or to refuse the troops she wanted. While he hesitated, more and more people throughout France heard of Joan. Yearning for a bold, confident leader, they pinned their hopes on her. Only a few skeptics mumbled, "Maybe she's deluded—and maybe by the devil himself."

Glad to have an excuse for delay, Charles chose learned prelates to examine her. The examination actually strengthened her position. The answers she gave proved her to be anything but a witch or a neurotic. Everyone marveled at the sturdy peasant girl's common sense, and they laughed at her wit. The opinion of the prelates was unanimous: they found in her "only humility, purity, honesty, and simplicity".

The people cheered the verdict. It reaffirmed their hope that God had chosen Joan to deliver them from English bondage and to bring peace at last to their warring land.

The verdict also persuaded Charles to take the unprece-

dented move of naming Joan as *chef de guerre*. Thus empow-
ered, her cry was "To Orleans!"

Men were marshaled, supplies were collected, and a march
toward the town began. Sadly, there was much bungling
on the part of Joan's captains, who ignored her explicit
orders. Some of the French knights grumbled that they did
not mind using Joan as a mascot or a morale booster, but
to take orders from "a wench of low degree", as one knight
called her, was another matter. The recalcitrance caused
needless delay but did not prevent the forts ringing Orleans
from falling like dominoes. Joan, in glistening white armor
and mounted on a white charger, led the army to attack time
after time and time after time to victory.

Only the big prize, Orleans, remained. But Joan, hoping
to avoid bloodshed, halted three days before the city while
she sent the English general daily letters demanding
surrender. With the third refusal, Joan cried, *"Avant!
Avant!"* and led the assault.

As the battle raged, an arrow pierced her armor above her
left breast and passed through her body, standing out (said
an eyewitness) "a hand's breadth beyond her shoulder".

When she was carried to the rear, the English, now sure
of victory, took heart. The French fought all day, but
without success. Though she wept with pain, Joan managed
to return to battle by sunset. Suddenly, the French caught
sight of her waving banner with its inscription "Jesu,
Marie", and they cheered lustily. Nothing could stop them
now. They charged forward as one man.

It was soon over. The French had won a great victory.
Church bells rang out, church choirs sang hymns of
thanksgiving, and townsfolk hugged one another, laughing
and crying for joy.

That night the English commander wrote home that the

French were aided by "a fiend called 'the Maid' who used false enchantment and sorcery".

Joan, coached by her voices, planned to follow up the martial victory by a psychological victory, the dauphin's crowning at Reims cathedral. But the ever-wavering Charles demurred, saying that since some towns en route were still enemy held, it would be hazardous to travel to Reims.

Joan's answer was, "I'll capture those towns", and she followed her words by the so-called "Eight Day Wonder", winning in eight days victories over more than eight towns, ending with Patay. The great victory at Patay destroyed English power in France, or as her biographer Mark Twain put it, "crippled the gigantic war that was ninety-one years old. At Orleans, she struck it a staggering blow, on the field of Patay she broke its back."

One of her captains said of her, "The positions she took were so admirable that the most experienced captains would not have made so good a plan", and another said, "All marveled how cautiously and with what foresight she went to work as if she had been a captain with twenty or thirty years' experience."

Some towns she did not have to attack. She would align her full army before each city's gates; then hoping to avoid bloodshed, she would demand surrender "by order of the King of Heaven in whose service the Maid spends her days". A few did surrender, one of them being Beauvais.

Beauvais' bishop, Pierre Cauchon, a venal prelate, served the English for reward. When Joan appeared, he lost his bishopric and his possessions and fled to Rouen, where later he was to wreak vengeance on the Maid.

Joan, whose mind was on the coming coronation, was at that time unaware of his existence. At last, standing in the vast cathedral at the dauphin's side, holding her banner aloft, she saw him crowned King Charles VII of France.

"On to Paris!" was Joan's next cry. But Charles, either treacherously or stupidly, signed a temporary truce with England's allies, the Burgundians, and Joan had to honor his solemn pledge. Meanwhile, the enemy, as Joan warned him they would, brought up reinforcements and strengthened defenses. It was a wonder that she did not quit the service of such a king. She had nothing to gain by continuing to fight for him; indeed, her voices told her that she had much to lose, for she would soon be captured. But Joan served God and country first and served Charles only incidentally.

When at last the truce expired, she was free to march toward Paris. At Compiègne, she met the enemy. The battle went badly, Joan received a slight wound, and the French, hotly pursued by Burgundians, sought refuge in a fort. When the commander thought the last Frenchman was within its stout walls, he raised the drawbridge. He did not realize that their leader, Joan, the last person to seek safety, was shut out. Instantly, she was surrounded and captured.

In those days, a captured person of rank was held for ransom, so Joan expected Charles to ransom her. Instead, he shrugged and ignored her. One biographer said, "No words can adequately describe Charles' disgraceful ingratitude and apathy."

Imprisoned in a tower, Joan heard that the Burgundians planned to sell her to the English. To avoid that fate, she essayed escape by rashly jumping from a window many feet from the ground. The fall knocked her unconscious. She was immediately recaptured and taken to the English prison of Rouen.

The English could not execute her for defeating them, so they needed to find her guilty of a crime that would seem to justify the death penalty. Since many believed, or wanted to believe, that she won victory by witchcraft, they planned to use that charge. But it would demand an ecclesiastical court. The English talked to the bishop of Beauvais, Pierre Cauchon. Since Joan's victory at Beauvais had lost him his sinecure there, he had no love for her, and he was glad to act as supreme judge and bring in the "proper" verdict— particularly since the English hinted they would then "arrange" that he be made archbishop of Rouen.

Eagerly he selected judges required by law to serve with him—men who were either as biased as he was, or who feared to oppose him, or who could be bribed. Then he illegally denied Joan counsel. The lone teenager must answer on her own whatever crafty questions sixty learned men could devise.

Her every word was recorded, so we know, not from romantic embroidery but from cold court evidence, how she answered. Her simplicity, her directness, her lucidity, her pluck, and her natural wit and wisdom foiled the wiles of her would-be entrappers. Time after time she bested them. For example, they asked her if she were in the state of grace. If she said No, she condemned herself; if she said Yes, she would be accused of sacrilegious presumption. She answered, "If I am, I pray God keep me in it. If I am not, I pray him put me in it."

As one biographer, Andrew Lang, said, "Her genius rose to every occasion." And the trial lasted three months, February 20 to May 30.

All day every day she wore heavy iron chains on her wrists and ankles, and at night additional chains bound her to the bed. In her prison room stood an iron cage in which she could be chained in an upright position, pinioned at the neck, waist, and ankles. Some chroniclers report that she was put in this cage in the beginning. The severe treatment, despite her robust health, brought on illness. Cauchon and her

English foes, afraid of losing the sweet revenge of seeing her die as a convicted witch, sent for a doctor, and she did recover.

Besides physical pain, there was mental and spiritual pain. She was denied news of her army, though her captains fought on with some success. (Strangely, none tried to rescue Joan.) But suspense and lack of news were minor compared to other torments. Her guards, five coarse, ribald English soldiers, refused her a moment's privacy, frequently made obscene jokes, used foul language, and, worst of all, attempted familiarities. To protect her virginity, she slept fully clothed and in male attire.

Then the heresy charge gave her captors an excuse to deprive her of the spiritual comfort of Mass and the sacraments. Repeatedly she asked Cauchon to lay her case before the Pope, and although her request was a right by law, he refused.

She won so much sympathy from the public and indeed from many of the judges that Cauchon moved the trial to the privacy of her prison room with just one or two judges he could trust to side with him. Still, she retained her spunk, and she told Cauchon boldly that her voices predicted final French victory.

Cauchon's verdict: her voices were "false and diabolical" and she was a "blasphemer".

Now the secular English court must pass sentence.

It was "Death by burning at the stake!"

Dressed uncharacteristically in women's garb, the nineteen-year-old girl was led out to the blazing fire. She stood there, feeling its scorching heat on her cheeks, while her judges, as required by law, urged her to save herself by repenting and signing a confession.

Weary and weakened by months of suffering, fear overcame her and she signed. She was led back to prison.

But Cauchon didn't intend her to escape death. One of the charges against her was wearing male attire, so if she resumed it, that would constitute a relapse and make her again liable to the death penalty. A court officer, tipstaff Jean Massieu, recorded that her jailers took away her woman's dress, and though she asked them for it, they refused to give it to her. When Cauchon visited her prison room, then, she was wearing male attire, and he declared, "You have condemned yourself."

She answered, "Bishop, I die because of you!"

At the stake again, her courage surged back. She knelt, prayed for her enemies, then asked for a cross. A sympathetic English soldier, sobbing convulsively, took two pieces of wood, joined them in a cross, and handed it to her.

Murmuring "Jesu", she placed the rude cross in her bosom and began to climb the scaffold to the stake as boldly as she had once climbed scaling ladders.

Someone laid a torch to the fagots. The flames leapt up. A sympathetic priest ran to a nearby church and fetched a crucifix that he held up before her. Now, except for the awful crackling of the fire, there was utter and unearthly silence. No one seemed to breathe. Then suddenly the stillness was shattered. Joan had cried out—no, not agonizingly—but exultantly, "Ah, my voices did not deceive me!"

Moments later she cried out again, "Jesu! Jesu!" and her head fell forward. She was dead.

The English king's secretary, a witness that day, was the first to speak. He exclaimed, "We have burned a saint!"

4

SHE GAVE US AMERICA

Isabella of Castile

(1451–1504)

Columbus might never have sailed westward and the history of our country might have been very different but for one woman. This woman, Queen Isabella, had the vision, the intuition, and the spirit given to the rare few.

But Isabella would have been a giant of the ages even if there had been no Columbus; indeed one biographer likened her feats to those of Charlemagne. She more than anyone else deserves credit for unifying Spain and making possible its Golden Age in history.

In the mid-fifteenth century when she was born, Spain was not a single kingdom. It was a cluster of small Christian kingdoms that sometimes warred among themselves, plus a Moorish kingdom, or caliphate, which often launched jihads, or "holy wars", against its Christian neighbors.

The blue-eyed, auburn-haired Isabella was a princess of Castile and Leon. When she was only three, her father died and her half brother, Henry (her father's son by a first marriage), mounted the throne. Isabella's mother, retiring to a small provincial town, reared Isabella and Isabella's infant brother, Alfonso, to pray devoutly, to live austerely, to study diligently, and to esteem religion and learning above worldly honors.

When Isabella was thirteen, Henry summoned the children to his court to complete their education there.

What a change! Henry's wife, the scheming, amoral Juana, was a far cry from the child's pious mother, while Henry himself was both a scoundrel and a weakling. His subjects had little respect for him, and since he had sired no heir to the throne, they inelegantly called him "Henry the Impotent".

Most people believed that a daughter whom Juana bore (although Henry required the usual oath of allegiance to her from his subjects) was not Henry's child but the child of Juana's lover, Don Beltran de la Cueva. The populace dubbed the child—and history knows her as—"La Beltraneja".

Juana feared that the people might rally around Alfonso and Isabella and declare them, rather than her daughter, the rightful heirs. There is a story (possibly apocryphal) that she once sent Alfonso a tempting fish dish. Before he tasted it, he threw a tidbit to his dog, whereupon the poor animal went into convulsions and quickly died.

At any rate, long disgusted with both Henry and Juana, many nobles now felt that something must be done. They drew up a document that declared La Beltraneja illegitimate and declared the boy, Alfonso, Henry's heir. The document also demanded that no marriage be arranged for Isabella without the consent of the three estates.

Although Henry signed the humiliating document when it was presented to him, he disregarded it when, a little later, he began marriage negotiations for Isabella. He chose for her Don Pedro Giron, master of the military Order of Calatrava, whom one writer (Lawrence Schoonover) described as "sensual, gluttonous, slothful, vain", and "given to decadent vice".

When Isabella protested the match, she was, by royal order, locked in the castle tower.

Isabella didn't spend hours in useless crying; devout as always, she prayed.

Some people said that what happened next had to be a miracle—or poison. Don Pedro, galloping toward his first meeting with his intended bride, suddenly doubled over in acute pain and within twenty-four hours was dead.

Henry released Isabella, and the nobles, furious that Henry had broken his word about consulting them, rose in arms against him. In an ensuing battle, they claimed victory. Then they arranged a dramatic ceremony. They dressed a dummy figure in sable robes and the archbishop, declaring Henry deposed, snatched the crown from the dummy's head, while the grandees took scepter and sword from its hands. Finally, they rolled the dummy in the dust. Alfonso was then led to the throne and crowned king.

Since Henry refused to abdicate, there were now two would-be kings, and the whole country was in turmoil.

Meanwhile, Henry and Juana whisked Isabella off to a fortress, where she was virtually a prisoner.

The boy king Alfonso had always been delicate, and the doctors' ministrations had never seemed to help him. Nonetheless, the gallant lad raised a small army and marched off to besiege the fortress and, like a fairytale prince, rescue the beautiful princess.

He succeeded, but shortly afterward, the delicate boy died. (Again came whispers, "Was it poison?")

The nobles now offered Isabella the crown. Amazingly, she refused it, saying, "As long as Henry lives, he is the rightful king. I will not divide the realm with civil war."

Her decision brought peace. The insurgents could not dethrone Henry when there was nobody to succeed him.

Henry was so grateful to Isabella that he, at her plea, granted amnesty to the rebels. He gave her the privilege— unheard of for a princess in those days—of choosing her own husband. And he acknowledged her as his heir, thereby admitting implicitly that La Beltraneja was not his daughter.

Now came marriage offers: from France's duke of Gui-
enne; from England's duke of Gloucester; from Portugal's
widower king; and from the neighboring kingdom of
Aragon's Prince Ferdinand.

Young, but wise, Isabella chose men from among those
who had now rallied around her and sent them to gather
information about her suitors. Ferdinand, the one nearest
her age, seemed to have the best intellectual and moral
qualifications.

Again from among her supporters, she chose a man versed
in law to draw up a marriage contract stipulating her
acceptance terms. Her husband must live in Castile; if she
succeeded to the throne, he must make no appointments,
civil, military, or ecclesiastical, without her consent; he and
she would sign all ordinances jointly and would hold equal
authority.

She sent the contract to Aragon by courier. Although it
was an unusual, if not an unprecedented document, giving
power to the queen equal to that of the king, Ferdinand
signed it, and Isabella announced her coming nuptials.

Now Henry, despite his promise to let her choose her
husband, threatened to imprison Isabella for insubordina-
tion, but the next morning when soldiers came to arrest her,
they could not get through the angry crowds. The nobles
carried swords and the common folk scythes, cleavers, and
butcher knives. They were ready to defend their "beautiful
princess" against the "wicked king". Henry had to rescind
the order for arrest.

Soon afterward, Henry went off on a military expedition
to the south, and Isabella sent word to Ferdinand to come
quickly while the coast was clear, and she added, "Come
secretly."

Ferdinand lost no time in setting out, and he and his scant
escort traveled disguised as peddlers, riding not their

accustomed horses but mules, and filling their saddlebags
with cheap pots and pans ostensibly for sale. To hide his
identity further, the shrewd Ferdinand acted as servant to
the little group. It was he who watered the mules when they
stopped at night; it was he who served the others at table
when they could find an inn.

When at length they came to the stronghold of one of
Isabella's partisans, the count of Trevino, they decided they
could safely declare themselves and so receive a cordial
welcome. It would be a relief to have hot food and soft beds!

But their disguise was too good. As they approached the
place, the sentinel, thinking Ferdinand and his escort were
highwaymen up to mischief, dropped a huge stone from the
battlement, calculated to kill. And kill it almost did! As
historian William Prescott said, it "glanced Ferdinand's
head".

On arrival at Valladolid, where Isabella awaited him,
Ferdinand changed into his formal velvet and satin robes and
presented himself at court. The ceremonious preliminaries
were scarcely over when the archbishop stepped forward,
urging the young couple to make their wedding arrangements pronto. He explained that Henry had learned of
Ferdinand's arrival and that he and his army were approach-
ing by forced marches to prevent the marriage.

Throughout the night, hammers flew as banners and
decorations were hastily put up in the cathedral. Finally, all
was ready for a morning wedding, but in the dim light of
dawn, Isabella was awakened and told, "Henry is within
sight of the city!"

Jumping out of bed, she quickly struggled into her
elaborate wedding gown with the help of her ladies-in-
waiting. Then when she met Ferdinand minutes later, he told
her there would be no time to go as far as the cathedral.

He had arranged for a wedding without Mass at a nearby chapel.

The "I do's" were soon spoken, and Ferdinand and Isabella were man and wife. Still no Henry! Well, why not go to the cathedral for the originally planned nuptial Mass?

The Mass proceeded with great dignity and decorum until the final benediction. Then, sudden uproar! Henry, flanked by his henchmen, had burst into the cathedral.

Isabella, turning to Ferdinand, said with a calm she probably did not feel, "Attend me, *mi Señor*", and taking his arm, she slowly walked down the aisle to meet Henry, curtsied, and said, "Your Highness, I present to you my husband."

Henry stood open mouthed and silent.

The young couple seemed to be happy and in love, although Isabella soon discovered that Ferdinand was rather cold and calculating and that he had a crafty streak.

Their first child was a daughter, and while she was still a toddler, they had reason to suspect a plot to kill her and themselves. As a precaution, they hurried to the fortress of Segovia. But Ferdinand did not stay immured long. His father sent word that the French had attacked Aragon, and Ferdinand felt he had to leave the stronghold to hasten to the aid of his sire.

In his absence, King Henry died, and almost immediately Isabella was crowned queen.

One of her first acts, in conjunction with Ferdinand, was to revive the *Santa Hermanidad*. During Henry's reign, criminals laughed at law, because punishment, though severe if it came, came only spasmodically. The *Santa Hermanidad* was a national police force, chosen from among the people, by the people. Members patrolled roads, apprehended wrongdoers, and imposed penalties as seemed appropriate to them. The *Hermanidad* was immensely popular because it curbed crime and protected the law-abiding.

There were many problems to solve. La Betraneja was now betrothed to the Portuguese king, who so recently had asked for Isabella's hand. He now attacked Castile, claiming that his wife-to-be, not Isabella, was heir to the throne. In the south, there was another Moorish uprising. Then the king of France, seeing Ferdinand and Isabella beset, seized the opportunity to attack from the north.

While Ferdinand fought on first one front, then another, Isabella, although pregnant, rode through the realm, raising troops and money, seeing that supplies were brought up, giving orders that roads be repaired when spring rains washed them out, personally supervising the transport of cannon over those roads, and directing strategy in places where Ferdinand could not be. Her people grew to know her well.

She was to go down in history as one of the most beloved queens of all time. William Prescott said (in his *History of Ferdinand and Isabella,* vol. 3) that her countrymen all but did her "homage as a titular saint".

But all the hours on horseback during that warring period had one disastrous effect: she suffered a miscarriage.

Then came another woe. Despite her almost mystic charisma, which inspired men to open up their coffers to her, the cost of the multipronged war still exceeded the gold so generously poured into the royal treasury. The situation seemed hopeless. If there was no money to pay for the war, the enemy would win by default.

Did Isabella pray for a miracle?

It almost seemed that one occurred when the primate of Spain, fearing the infidel Moors would take advantage of the situation and that Christian Spain would suffer, made an unprecedented offer: he would order that one-third of all sacred vessels and reliquaries throughout Castile be melted down and their gold given to the crown. Isabella could repay him in three years without interest. For security, her word was enough.

Though immensely grateful for his offer, Isabella demurred. Wouldn't some prelates resent the order and seek to evade it by burying their gold? She suggested to the primate that he ask the other prelates to meet in convocation and take a vote so that they would have a voice in the move.

He accepted her suggestion, the vote was "Aye", and pronto Isabella had gold!

Victory followed victory, and always Ferdinand was in the thick of battle, fighting lustily—and luckily; he never received so much as a scratch.

The French and the Moors capitulated, and only the Portuguese fought on, but irregularly. Isabella, with more time for domestic affairs, revived the *Audencias,* informal courts of law where she and the king sat as judges and to which anyone, high or low, could bring a grievance. Like the *Hermanidad,* the *Audencias* were extremely popular, because Isabella's decisions were always wise and fair.

About this time, the king of Aragon, Ferdinand's aged father, died. Ferdinand hurried off to receive the Aragon crown.

In his absence, Isabella met with the sister-in-law of the Portuguese king and worked out a peace treaty, which was ratified by the court in Lisbon. When Ferdinand returned, he applauded Isabella's peacemaking coup, but at the same time he was piqued that she had acted independently of him on so grave a matter.

He was placated and happy soon after, however, when she bore him a son, and less happy again a year later when she bore another child who seemed slightly backward. (This was the princess who eventually became known as "Joanna the Mad".)

Then, too, he was annoyed that Isabella questioned establishing the Inquisition in Castile; it took interminable urging to overcome her reluctance. He wanted to get rid of the infidel Moors, the heretic Christians, and the crypto-Jews, who, he believed, were often disloyal and subversive. Besides, he argued, the fines and the confiscated property would raise money to pay the debt to the cardinal.

Isabella would have liked to convert the infidels, heretics, and Jews—she had a special catechism written to that end; as for raising money, she had an idea there too. Her predecessor, Henry, had been improvident and careless. It had tickled his ego to bestow royal gold, crown lands, and castles on his favorites, although by doing so he violated his coronation oath to guard and defend them. (Because of this illegal generosity he had sometimes been called "El Liberal".)

Isabella's idea was to convene the *Cortes,* or legislature, since many of its members had received Henry's bounty, and to have these members vote on whether or not the property should be returned to the crown. She herself addressed them: "If you had . . . told me that our predecessor had unlawfully deprived *you* of certain estates . . . *I* would have restored them to you."

Her sincerity was patent. Moreover, they knew that the populace resented their irregularly acquired wealth and, loving Isabella as it did, it would take it ill if her plea was resisted. They voted to restore the wealth.

Suddenly, the royal coffers bulged! Isabella now had a surplus, and she spent it in novel ways: for pensions for widows of slain soldiers, for settling veterans on little farms carved from the crown lands, for the planting of thousands of trees to stop soil erosion, and for raising the pay of university professors. (Incidentally, in a most unusual move, she appointed several women professors.)

Isabella's active mind was always trying to solve problems. Her *Audencias* experience was proving that the nation's laws needed codification and, above all, simplification. She appointed an eminent legal scholar to undertake the monumental task. After much painstaking work, he produced *Ordencas,* which Isabella had "printed in types". (She was extremely enthusiastic about the new invention of printing presses, and she encouraged the establishment of printing presses in every part of Spain.)

But it was Isabella's next accomplishments, expelling the Moors and backing Columbus, that electrified the world.

The Moors attacked and captured a frontier town. Many Christian prisoners were taken and thrown into dungeons. As usual, Ferdinand was ready to march off and punish the Moors. But Isabella said, "This must not be a short, quick, retaliatory move. It must be a war that puts an end to the sporadic fighting that goes on year after year, century after century. It must be a war that will drive the Moors from Spain forever and unite our whole land into one Christian kingdom."

Ferdinand, though no friend of the Moors and though certainly not lacking in bravery, thought her grand aim unrealistic and at first shrugged it off.

Over seven centuries before, Arab Muslims had invaded from North Africa and the Middle East. (At first they were called simply Arabs; the name *Moor* came centuries later.) They had swarmed into Spain and taken over the country. Then, beginning with the fabled warrior El Cid, Christians slowly forced the Moors back until they held only the kingdom of Granada. But of late, Christians had contented themselves mostly with raids and skirmishes, although not long before Isabella's coronation, a grandee in fierce fighting had captured "impregnable" Gibraltar.

Now at Isabella's call, men everywhere joined together to fight the "infidel Moor". She was again in the saddle hours on end. Ferdinand led on the battlefields; Isabella did everything from planning strategy to seeing that her court physician set up hospital tents behind the lines. (These were considered the earliest camp hospitals on record.) Washington Irving called her "the soul of the war against the Moors".

She kept up this pace until the last months of another pregnancy. She called the new baby Catherine. (This Catherine of Aragon would later marry England's Henry VIII.)

While the war raged, Columbus entered the scene. Although others had been leery of his proposed venture (including the rulers of Genoa, Portugal, and Venice), it fired Isabella's imagination. But Ferdinand, ever cool and wary, distrusted its practicality; at most he agreed to appoint a commission of astronomers and cosmographers to examine Columbus.

This erudite group were loathe to learn from a man without academic honors, who challenged many long-held assumptions. As historian Las Casas wrote, "Before Columbus could make his solutions and reasoning understood . . . he had to . . . remove from his auditors those erroneous principles on which their objections were founded, a task always more difficult than teaching doctrine."

The commission reported that the attainment of Columbus' aim seemed all but impossible to "an educated person".

Columbus again tried to apply directly to the Spanish sovereigns, but the demands of war precluded an audience. At last, discouraged, he wrote other sovereigns. The Portuguese king replied that he might reconsider his earlier unfavorable decision, and Henry VII of England replied by inviting Columbus to his court. Still, Columbus lingered in Spain. Historian Washington Irving wrote, "There must have been strong hopes authorized . . . by the Spanish sovereigns to induce Columbus to neglect these invitations."

Yet for seven months, Isabella and Ferdinand were seemingly oblivious of Columbus, as they besieged the Moorish capital, Granada. Then dawned the day when Columbus saw with his own eyes the sultan surrender his crown into the hands of Spanish sovereigns—the act that ended 778 years of Moorish occupation of strongholds on Spanish soil, the act that transformed Spain from a conglomerate of petty kingdoms into one strong, Christian nation. The cross went up, the crescent of Islam came down.

Soon afterward Columbus had his audience.

It dashed his hopes. Although trade was picking up and obviously great prosperity lay ahead, Ferdinand still winced at financing the venture. Besides, as Professor Samuel Morison wrote in his biography of Columbus, Ferdinand was interested "only in European wars and in diplomacy". Isabella pleaded Columbus' cause, but she failed to sway her husband, so she accepted his decision and Columbus was dismissed.

He left the royal presence never expecting to return. He had not gone far when Isabella had second thoughts. She averred, "I will undertake this enterprise for my own crown. I pledge my jewels to raise the funds."

She sent a courier after Columbus, who overtook the great man on the bridge of Pinos on his way out of the country.

Yes, Isabella gave us America! She was indeed a fabulous female. And Washington Irving in his biography of Columbus said, "She is one of the purest and most beautiful characters in the pages of history."

Columbus sailed on August 3, 1492, from Palos and discovered America on October 12, the day that the feast of Our Lady of Pilar is celebrated in Spain.

The rest of Isabella's life is rather sad and seems anticlimactic. Her son John died, her daughter Catherine was repudiated by her husband Henry VIII for Anne Bolyn, and her daughter Joanna went mad. Still, Isabella continued to work on. In 1503 she organized the secretariat of Indian affairs to protect the Indians against ill usage by some of the Spaniards. She became patroness of Cisneros, the churchman who worked toward monastic reform in Spain under the authority of Pope Alexander VI.

Isabella died at age fifty-three, and Ferdinand promptly remarried.

5

SOARING EAGLE

Teresa of Ávila

(1515–1582)

The English poet Richard Crashaw called Teresa an eagle—
and she was that indeed, for she soared far beyond "the many
headed multitude" of mankind.

Although throughout its ages-long history the Catholic
Church had never before honored a woman with the title
"Doctor of the Church", it so honored Teresa, for her
books, among the world's greatest works on mysticism,
eminently deserved that recognition. Then her Reform
Movement was stupendous; it not only changed the face of
her native country but also had repercussions beyond it.

Born in Spain in the early sixteenth century, this
whirlwind of energy and zeal, this embodiment of charm
and charisma, this whole-hearted, ardent flame of love, this
reformer with a sense of humor convinced numerous lax-
living, earthly minded nuns and monks in the Spain of her
day to seek the "perfect gifts" from above. Seemingly, she
went through the land with a torch and everywhere
rekindled the spirits of religious in convents and monasteries

Largely because of the changes she made, the Protestant
Reformation had a feebler impact on Spain than on the rest
of Europe. And through her books, she has been changing
and influencing people ever since. These books, translated
into many languages, are still read avidly four centuries after
her death.

She was born in the beautiful, austere northern province of Old Castile. Her father, Don Alonso de Cepeda, and her mother, Dona Beatriz Davila y Ahumada, were both of the nobility. Since Spanish custom sanctions a child taking as surname either the surname of the father or the maiden name of the mother, Teresa used for her surname her mother's maiden name Ahumada.

Teresa, a bright, lively child with a mischievous twinkle in her dark eyes, led a carefree and comfortable life with her large family of siblings. She was usually the ringleader in their play, and she had an adventurous streak. When she was quite tiny, she persuaded one of her brothers to run away from home with her. She had the romantic notion that they could go to North Africa, "the land of the Moors", be killed for the Faith, become glorious martyrs, and then march into heaven to the blare of trumpets.

Alas, an uncle saw the two tykes trudging along the road and brought them back home, tired and hungry after walking a mile.

Then Teresa decided they could be hermits, and although they had no handy desert, she said they could make do by building a hermitage in the garden. They had piled up just about the last stone of the hermitage's walls when it collapsed thunderingly into a heap at their feet.

Teresa's happy childhood came to an end at age fourteen when her mother died. Sobbing, the girl begged the Blessed Mother to be her mother.

But youth is resilient, and Teresa, who was blossoming into an attractive young lady, took to reading avidly every tale of chivalry she could find, no doubt imagining herself as the courted lady love of some gallant knight. She began to be interested in pretty clothes and in all sorts of frills and fripperies. In her own words, "I began to deck myself out and try to attract others by my appearance, taking great trouble with my hands and hair, perfume, and all the vanities I could get."

Her pious father, seeing this, probably thought that he, a lone widower, needed a little help with her upbringing, so he sent her off to a school run the by Augustinians in their convent.

Once there, Teresa saw that she had indeed been a bit frivolous; she should start thinking seriously of what she wanted to do with her life. She wasn't sure she wanted to get married, but she knew for certain she didn't want to be a nun.

Then, a year and a half later, still at the Augustinian school, she became ill. When she was somewhat better, her father decided to send her to a married sister's home to recuperate. To break the journey for the still-weak girl, he arranged for a stop of a few days en route at the home of an uncle.

While she was with her uncle, he asked her several times to read aloud to him from a spiritual book. It had arresting ideas. Much later, Teresa was to write in her famous "Bookmark" the words "All things pass away; God only shall stay." But the thought itself struck her at this time, and she began to reason: if God alone lasts, I'd better put him first. Serving him is all that's going to matter in the long run.

Then Teresa's thoughts went on: clearly, many roads lead to heaven, but the surest road, and the shortest, lies through the cloister. To play safe, I'd be smart to take it.

It all seemed logical—but not enticing. Who wanted to become a nun? Not she! However, she gritted her teeth and decided she would be sensible and become a nun anyhow.

Later she was to write, "You have only one soul; you have only one death; you have only one life to live, which is short and which has to be lived by you alone, and there is only one glory that counts, and that is eternal."

Once having screwed up the courage to enter the convent, Teresa decided to act quickly before she had a change of heart. But, surprisingly, her father objected. He said she seemed unfitted for the cloister; this was just her latest romantic notion. Besides, he didn't want to part with her, especially since one of her older sisters had recently married and left home. His directive was, "Don't enter now. If you still want to after I'm dead, then go ahead."

But Teresa was afraid that if she waited, her resolve might waver, so again she ran away from home.

One biographer said she wore a red dress on that day, and somehow the vivid color seems exactly right for Teresa. As she breathlessly hurried along the dusty road, she perhaps wondered if she would make it to the nearby convent, or if her father would, like her uncle of old, espy her and bring her back home.

Well, she made it, and although when she arrived the nuns sent word to her father of her presence, she stayed. Her father sighed and accepted the fait accompli.

She had gone to the Carmelite Convent of the Incarnation just outside the walls of Ávila. Once there, instead of finding the new life dull as she had expected, she found it a challenge, a stimulus, and—yes—a joy. She wrote later, "This life gave me a joy so great that it has never failed me."

And she found that instead of giving up treasure, she received treasure for, as she put it, "He who has God, has ALL."

In time Teresa made her vows, donned the veil and habit, and became Sister Teresa of Jesus. She was content.

Then unexpectedly she fell ill—far more seriously ill than before. Obviously, in sixteenth-century Europe, scientific knowledge was far sparser than it is today, and doctors couldn't diagnose her malady. However, that didn't stop them from prescribing treatments and medicines that were useless or harmful. Meanwhile, poor Teresa was in great pain.

Her worried and distressed father now insisted on her coming home; he resolved to take her to a woman who had a reputation for effecting many cures.

En route to the woman's infirmary, Teresa stopped, as on the previous journey, at the home of her uncle. Again the pious man plied her with spiritual books, and again the books influenced her deeply. Using one particular treatise as a guide, Teresa essayed meditative prayer. Until then, she said, "I didn't know how to practice prayer, or how to recollect myself."

Now she saw that prayer was not just addressing words to God. It was an orientation toward God; it was an awareness of God's presence in her soul, as a person is aware of another person in the same room, even though she may be busy reading, writing, sewing, or whatever.

Teresa's new prayer life gave her strength to go on from day to day, and she needed strength, for she was in much pain. As she suffered, she could think of—and really understand something of—her Lord's excruciating suffering as he hung (and still hangs in the eternal NOW) from nails through his hands and his feet. In a very real sense, she suffered with him, and he suffered with her, helping her to bear the pain.

The pain had not lessened by the time she reached the infirmary. Treatment there brought no relief; on the contrary, it made her worse.

Her father, now afraid Teresa might soon die, snatched her away and took her, not back to the convent, but to his home.

That move didn't help either. In fact, Teresa lapsed into a coma, and everyone thought at first she had died.

Although the coma did not last long and Teresa opened

her eyes again, no one believed that her pitiable condition
was improved; they awaited her death.

At this point she asked to be taken back to the Incarnation
where she could die in the convent she had chosen for her
home. The short journey there seemed like a funeral
procession, but in reality it marked a turning point of the
disease, for she was scarcely back before she began to
improve, and she continued to improve as the days passed.
Possibly the disease had run its course. Or possibly the lack
of treatments helped her. And certainly prayer helped. She
had been begging God, through the intercession of St.
Joseph, to cure her.

She recovered enough to lead not only a normal life but
eventually an ultra-strenuous life, although some impair-
ment of her health lasted the rest of her days. Certainly,
too, she recovered enough to regain her high spirits, and
soon she was enjoying herself with those around her.

And because of her natural magnetism, she always had
people around her. She spent far more time laughing and
joking and visiting in the parlor with friends and family than
she spent on her knees in the chapel. The mental prayer she
had begun to practice during illness was now a haphazard
practice that filled time when nothing else beckoned.

The days passed pleasantly enough until word came that
Teresa's father was ill. Since the style of life in the cloister
in those days didn't discourage nuns from coming and going
almost at will, the Mother Superior readily agreed to
Teresa's going home for an indefinite time.

Worried about her father's health, Teresa resumed prayer.
She prayed more often and more earnestly than she had in
a long time. But it still wasn't the consistent, wordless
awareness of God or the wordless or the spoken reaching
out to him with mind and heart. For fairly long intervals,
she would ignore him as she became absorbed in the affairs

of her family and friends. Still, when she did pray, she found
comfort, and she needed it, for her father grew worse and
finally died.

In that long visit home, Teresa declared that she was trying
to live two lives, that of a nun and that of a worldling. She
didn't manage the dual role very adroitly. Much later she
wrote of this period, saying, "On the one hand God was
calling me. On the other hand, I was following the world.
All the things of God gave me pleasure, yet I was tied and
bound to those of the world. . . . I spent many years in this
way, and now I am amazed that a person could have gone
on for so long without giving up either the one or the other."

God, "hound of Heaven" that he is, kept pursuing Teresa
until something happened—she called it "conversion".
Anyway, she came to the point where, in her own words,
"I understood what a great blessing it is to set no store by
anything that will not bring us closer to God." She decided
then that she must stop the foolish straddling of the two
worlds and give herself and her life once and for all entirely
to him.

That decision made, she felt free and light and happy. She
was to write at a later date, "As soon as the soul empties
itself of self for the love of God, the Lord fills it with
*him*self."

It was like falling in love—in fact it *was* falling in love
with God. She pitied those who did not love God, and she
defined Satan as "that poor wretch who cannot love".

Because Teresa had great capacity for love, her falling in
love with God revolutionized her life. God responded to her
ardor by showing her openly that he loved her too. He often
appeared to her, and often he spoke to her and she could
hear his distinct words, whether or not she could see him.

Although all this was an exultant joy, it was frightening.
She never sought these marvels, and she wrote, "The highest

perfection consists, not in . . . great raptures, nor in visions, nor in the spirit of prophecy, but in the bringing of our wills so closely into conformity to the will of God that as soon as we realize he wills anything, we will it ourselves with all our might and take the bitter with the sweet."

But the supernatural phenomena upset Teresa for a second reason; she felt unworthy of them. Oh yes, saints sometimes were so favored, but who was she? She said to herself, "Frivolous me has a thousand silly faults. How can God favor me? Maybe the devil is playing tricks. Or am I having hallucinations?"

Obviously, what this young girl considered sins or faults would seem nothing to the rest of us. But since she was worried, she consulted theologians and asked their opinion.

Not wanting to be hasty, they ordered her to write an account of her spiritual life and its experiences.

The resulting book, now called simply *A Life of St. Teresa of Jesus,* was not only an account of what had happened but a treatise on prayer that is considered one of the finest books of its kind ever written. A modern biographer said, "Only *The Confessions of St. Augustine* can bear comparison with it."

While Teresa was writing the book, she realized more keenly than ever before that the worldly atmosphere at the Convent of the Incarnation discouraged prayer.

Traditional Carmelites had always insisted on some solitude in which to seek communion with God. Old tales told that from Elijah's time, a group of men known as Carmelites (because they lived in caves on the slopes of Palestine's Mt. Carmel) led a hermitlike life while seeking communion with God. They met only for occasional group prayer. After Christ's coming, Christians joined them, but it wasn't until the year 1247 that a Rule was formally drawn up defining their style of life. About 100 years before Teresa's time, in 1432 (the Carmelite Order having spread to Europe and having acquired a female as well as a male branch), the Pope mitigated this "Primitive Rule", making it less austere. Then, as time passed, the Carmelites themselves kept easing restrictions in the Rule until some thought it self-indulgent.

Incarnation had 140 nuns in a smallish building, so no one could escape a hum of conversation at all hours. Someone called the place "a chirping birdcage of femininity".

Then visitors, including men friends, regularly came to see the nuns. Girls who had not found an eligible marriage partner, but who did not want to stay home under parental supervision, and widows who could not easily maintain a home alone in the sort of society that sixteenth-century Europe provided—all of these single women, as well as those whose primary aim was to seek God, might enter a convent. Convents then were often like modern women's clubs, where members were permanent guests.

This was not Teresa's idea of a life led close to God. Having written about meditative and contemplative prayer and struggling to practice it regularly, she was now convinced that God was demanding it of her and of many others. But unless the Primitive Rule were revived, how achieve the silence, the solitude, and the other-worldly atmosphere necessary for such prayer?

One day she said as much to one of her cousins, who answered, "Why not found your own convent? I'll supply money for a house."

It *was* an idea. Teresa thought about it and prayed about it. Then the Lord spoke, giving her, she said, "explicit commands to work for this with all my might".

Her black eyes sparkling with enthusiasm, Teresa approached the Carmelite provincial to get his endorsement of her idea. When she easily won him over and he told her to go ahead, she acted quickly. She found a house and was about to buy it when the provincial sent word that he had reconsidered because complaints had reached his ears. The nuns at Incarnation were up in arms. They were insulted that Teresa thought them too lax and too worldly, and they felt that a new convent would be a reflection on them. Nor were the townspeople happy. Would they be expected to support two Carmelite convents? One was enough, heaven knows! Where was the money to come from?

Apparently, the idea was to die aborning, so Teresa, thinking this God's will, tried to accept her disappointment gracefully. However, her cousin wrote to Rome petitioning for a brief that would authorize the foundation. The brief came, and again Teresa acted quickly: she founded the now-famed St. Joseph Convent in Ávila. She had with her four nuns, all anxious to lead a truly contemplative life. The date was August 24, 1562.

Soon applicants for admission were knocking at the convent gates, and the little building filled up quickly. Still applicants kept coming.

Since Teresa had seen that a crowd fostered sociability, not recollection, the only solution seemed to be another foundation—except that another foundation meant more money. Where get that?

Throughout her life from now on, that question was always answered by friends who stepped forward with money for a new foundation. During the next years, Teresa made foundation after foundation, because the fire of her enthusiasm convinced so many people that seeking God in quiet prayer and loving contemplation was the greatest of adventures and, more important, a pursuit that greatly pleased the heart of a loving God.

When the general of the Order visited Ávila, he was amazed and delighted by the deeply spiritual communities Teresa had founded. He told her to found convents throughout Castile—"as many as there are hairs on your head".

The longer that Teresa went on with this work of the "Reform", the more clearly she saw that if her nuns (the Descalced, the shoeless, as they were called because they wore only sandals) were to persevere in their efforts to live by the strict Primitive Rule, they should have for confessors and spiritual directors, Carmelite friars who also tried to follow the same Rule. She asked the general's permission to establish monasteries for men under the Primitive Rule.

A woman to found a man's Order! He was struck speechless.

However, Teresa had an engaging way that arose not only from her natural charm but also from a spiritual light shining through her, so the provincial ended by saying, in effect, "Go ahead and see if you have any luck."

To his surprise, she soon found two friars—an odd couple. One was a big strapping man, the other a short, little runt of a fellow, so Teresa joked, "I have found a friar and a half."

The little man was to prove her staunchest ally, and she grew to love him like a son. This man, who took the name John of the Cross, became her partner working for the Reform. He had been a follower of the mitigated Rule, but worldliness and lack of fervor in his community had made him unhappy, and he had planned to switch to the Carthusian Order. Then Teresa talked to him and said in effect, "Oh no! Remain a Carmelite. But work for the reform of the men's monasteries."

Talking to many people and trying to spark them with the love for God that would make them eager to cast aside comforts and conviviality for an austere, strictly God-centered life was time consuming, energy draining, and often aroused hostility. Then, too, Teresa had to find proper housing with scant funds—although surprisingly she turned out to be a shrewd businesswoman whose sharp eye could spot a bargain. But worst of all by far was the traveling from place to place. That meant jolting along in a mule-drawn cart that boasted no springs, mile after wearisome, bone-bruising mile. It meant, too, that Teresa and the nuns with her often missed meals when they trekked across arid plains or slowly struggled up rugged mountains. It meant that they were all but roasted under a hot summer sun and all but frozen under blasts of winter winds or snowstorms. Often, too, it meant that the fastidious Teresa, who considered cleanliness next to godliness, had to sleep in a flea-infested inn on filthy, smelly straw that littered the floor.

Still, she went on and on, and she kept her traveling companions amused and in good humor by her natural joie de vivre. She said once, "Lord deliver me from frowning saints", and her belief in prayerful hours of solitude didn't preclude her belief that there should be some intervals of sheer fun. She was known on occasion to dance for her nuns, whirling about with tambourine in her uplifted hand, her dark eyes sparkling all the while. Once only is it recorded that she complained to the Lord of hardship, and he said, "This is how I treat my friends." She answered with her dry humor, "Well Lord, that's why you have so few."

Even when she stayed for a while in a convent, she didn't and couldn't rest. Her sister nuns and her spiritual directors, impressed by her autobiography, kept asking her to write a second book. So at their request, she picked up her quill and wrote from day to day the thoughts that she lived by, the thoughts that God had sent her in prayer.

The result was the book now known as *The Way of Perfection*. Commenting about it, one biographer said, "Teresa writes with disarming naturalness and simplicity" in a "homely familiar style". She writes as though she were talking to a close friend.

How she ever wrote this particular book, which is a classic even more profound than her *Life,* is a mystery, for there were long interruptions when she had to establish or manage a new convent. No wonder she joked about writing "with both hands at once so as not to forget one thing while saying another".

The book had great influence on her Descalced nuns, and the papal nuncio was so impressed by the spirituality and the fervor that these women evinced that he told Teresa to found houses in other provinces of Spain beyond Castile. Since, in the hierarchical order, he outranked the general of the Order, who had sanctioned foundations only in Castile, Teresa naturally followed his directive.

There were difficulties ranging from lack of money to lack of recruits, but Teresa always seemed to have what she needed when the time came. On one occasion, she needed permission of the civil authorities to open a new convent, and an official wrote Teresa refusing the permission. One defeat at least?

No, she asked the official to meet her and give the refusal in person. He did meet her but he gave no refusal; she won him over.

Her unfailing success irked those Carmelites who still clung to the easier Rule. They complained to the general of the Order, "*Dios mio!* The woman has gone too far."

He agreed, for he was miffed that when he had sanctioned foundations only in Castile, Teresa was ranging far and wide. He decreed, "No more foundations anywhere", and he ordered all houses founded without his express permission closed forthwith. Then he sent Teresa to one of the older convents and said, "Never set foot outside its walls again."

He even imposed heavy penances on the Carmelite friars who had adopted Teresa's Reform.

Now why didn't the nuncio speak up to say that he had told Teresa to do exactly what she was doing? Well, just as the General of the Order was hurling his thunderbolts, the Nuncio died. His successor took his cue from the General and endorsed the harsh measures. Indeed, he went further; he denounced Teresa as a "gadabout" and had the Inquisition imprison her.

The Calced (or well-shod) friars, who resented Teresa's Reform as much as had the Calced nuns, now saw a chance for revenge; they seized John of the Cross, threw him into a narrow, stifling cell, and treated him cruelly. For nine long months he endured a distressful life, and he believed that it was only through the Blessed Mother's help that he managed to escape.

Now it seemed that the Reform had collapsed and all of Teresa's laborious work, like the work of building the stone walls of her childhood hermitage, had crashed in a heap.

But she wasn't really downcast. She had worked solely to please God, and God judged a work not by outward success but by the amount of love that went into it. Besides, he could turn failure to success. Meanwhile, she prayed and she wrote, producing among other works her greatest book of mystical theology, the superb *Interior Castle*.

Moreover, she had time to reflect about the Reform, and she saw that if it were to succeed, then the Calced and the Descalced must be completely separate. She wrote letters to those who might help effect the separation. One letter went to Spain's King Philip II. After all, this matter of many convents and monasteries touched a large number of his subjects. Since Teresa's detractors had practically shouted from the housetops outrageous and scandalous tales about her, Philip had heard the uproar and was curious enough to invite her to his court so that he could judge her personally. During the royal audience, she persuaded Philip that she had a case that was at least worth looking into. He appointed four men to meet with the nuncio, hear arguments from each side, and make an impartial decision.

The decision was in Teresa's favor, and she was authorized to continue her Reform by making foundations for Descalced nuns and friars. Then Descalced friars were released from the penances and told to form themselves into a separate province with their own leader, or provincial.

All of this was later officially confirmed by papal brief.

So work went on. Between 1567 when she began and 1582 when she died, Teresa made thirty-two foundations, seventeen for nuns, fifteen for friars.

In 1582, after making her last foundation at Burgos at the age of sixty-seven, she left the cathedral town and went to Alba de Tormes, where she realized she was more than tired; she was ill. She said to her sister companion gleefully, "At last! I've reached death."

Oh yes, death called for glee. Like a young girl in love, she longed to see her Love and her Lord. She had once exclaimed, " I die because I cannot die."

Now it seemed the big moment had come, and she told the Lord, "It's time that you and I saw each other."

Evidently, he agreed with her. Her last words were, "I am a daughter of the Church."

She was however no ordinary daughter of the Church. One of her foremost modern biographers, the Englishman Alison Peers, called her "one of the most remarkable women who ever lived by virtue of her character, her teaching, her gifts as a woman of affairs and as a writer" of twelve books. He called her a saint, too, for of course she was that, and she was officially canonized thirty years after her death in 1622 by Pope Gregory XV.

6

FOREVER UNFORGETTABLE

Mary Queen of Scots

(1542–1587)

Many potentates may be dead and forgotten, but not Mary Queen of Scots. She lives on in song and in legend.

Her story is set in an era of religious upheaval and bitterness. Even though she sometimes in her private life let her emotions rule her head, in her public life she was a judicious, fair, and broad-minded sovereign. In the end she was magnificent—she refused to repudiate her Faith to save her neck, so her violent death seems a triumph as well as a tragedy.

Her mother was the French Marie de Guise, whom Henry VIII of England once sought to marry. When the British king remarked on Marie's "fine stature" (she was tall and graceful), Marie, remembering that Henry had beheaded his second wife, Anne Boleyn, declared, "My neck is too slender for me to marry Henry."

James V of Scotland became her husband.

The two little sons of this union died quickly, and then Mary was born. Rejoicing at the baby's birth was turned into consternation and grief when word came that her father had died unexpectedly. The infant became a queen at six days old. She was only nine months old when she was solemnly crowned and given the sword and scepter.

Her first marriage proposal came when she was three months old. Henry VIII of England by this time had a son (the short-lived Edward), borne by his third wife, Jane Seymour, so he proposed the future marriage of the prince to Mary.

Before this matter was settled, the French royal couple, Henri II and Catherine de Medici, also parents of a son, proposed a future match for Mary with their son.

This competition led the English king to send forces headed by the earl of Hertford to Scotland with orders to kidnap Mary, and so the poor child had to be shunted from castle to castle, from stronghold to stronghold to hide her whereabouts.

When the kidnap venture failed, Henry VIII told Hertford (later known as the Scourge of the Scots) to inflict "all misery" by devastating Scottish territory and to put to the sword all resisters, be they men, women, or children. This so-called "Rough Wooing" ended unsuccessfully for Henry on "Black Saturday" with a bloody battle.

The Scots knew that Henry hoped to annex Scotland to his dominions through Mary. Therefore, although many Protestants, led by John Knox, opposed the French-Catholic marriage, others preferred it to the English, and it was approved. To safeguard Mary, her mother Marie reluctantly parted with the child, then only five years old, and sent her to the French court.

In France Mary was surrounded with every luxury, and, more important, the French king and queen treated her with genuine love and kindness. However, she led a disciplined life. Her days were spent in study and in various types of training, such as mastering the lute, equestrian skills, needlework, and so on. Fortunately, she enjoyed acquiring knowledge, and at a young age she eagerly studied Latin, Greek, poetry, history, mathematics, and other subjects. She was so well behaved and quick to learn that the cardinal of Lorraine wrote to her mother in Scotland, "Your

daughter is so perfect and accomplished in all things . . .
that the like of her is not to be seen in all the realm."

After two years Marie was able to visit her little daughter,
but not for long. She had to hurry back to Scotland to
safeguard Mary's throne there, for ambitious nobles as well
as the English sovereign were ready to pounce if opportunity
arose. Then Catholics and Protestants fought one another
and struggled for power with a bitterness than almost split
the country in two. Marie (another liberated lady) held
Scotland together for nine years until her death.

Meanwhile, in France Mary was growing up. Because she
had long since been a crowned queen, court etiquette
demanded that she take precedence over the French royal
children. Catherine de Medici, although kind to Mary, was
never quite happy about this. Henri II hardly seemed to
notice. He was extremely fond of Mary, and he treated her
with exactly the same affection as he did his own children.
Mary herself dearly loved every member of the French
royal family, and it seemed only natural and fitting to her
when the time came for her to marry the dauphin François.

The wedding was celebrated with the utmost pomp and
ceremony in Notre Dame cathedral. Beautiful, strawberry-
blonde Mary was a queenly bride, not only in appearance
but in fact. She was queen of Scotland, future queen of
France, and, according to Catholics, indisputably the actual,
though unacknowledged, queen of England. Elizabeth, who
sat on the English throne, was considered of illegitimate
birth by those who did not countenance Henry VIII's
divorce from his first wife. Illegitimate children in that era
never succeeded to the throne.

Henri II of France had the English royal arms engraved
on Mary's seal and plate, embroidered on her tapestry, and
emblazoned on her carriages. No one can say where this
might have led if Henri had lived much longer. In the festive

games and tournaments that followed Mary's wedding, the king was anxious "to break a lance or two". This he did with élan until he was accidentally struck in the temple by a lance and killed.

Suddenly, Mary was queen of France! Her young husband was king, but he disliked and feared his royal responsibilities. He had always been frail; moreover, he was not interested in learning statescraft, in studying history, and certainly not in reading legal documents. Mary, with help and advice from her Guise uncles, tried to rule France. She did amazingly well.

Not long after she began to reign, the sad news came that her mother had died. Then the political situation in Scotland worsened overnight. It was an era when religion seemed to be politics, and politics seemed to be religion. The Scottish Parliament, without consulting or seeking the consent of their queen in France, had declared Protestantism the state religion. This meant that adherents to the Catholic religion, which their sovereign practiced, were breaking the law.

Before the girl queen of seventeen could consider counteraction, François became suddenly and seriously ill. Within a few short days, he died. Mary, who had been very fond of him, was deeply grieved.

The death of François demoted Mary from queen consort to queen dowager; she had no more real power. Another of Catherine's sons was now king. Still, Mary remained an important personage. She was queen of Scotland, dowager queen of France, claimant to the English throne, and she had the option of remarriage that could bolster her position. Her Guise uncles opened negotiations to arrange a marriage for her to the Spanish royal heir, Don Carlos, and Spain at that time was the most powerful country in Europe.

But Scotland was Mary's prime duty. Much as she loved France, she believed she should return to her native land, where she could better discharge her responsibilities as queen.

The Spanish negotiations broke off. The Spanish king, Philip, wanted to see how things proceeded in Scotland for Mary, remarking, "I don't want to marry my son to a process."

On her landing, Scottish nobles met her and paid her homage, but many of them, Catholic as well as Protestant, had a self-serving motive; they hoped by a show of loyalty to win personal advantage. It was the populace that really took Mary to its heart. The people staged welcoming festivals and street carnivals. When she made it a point to thank everyone graciously for the least little attention, they were immensely pleased. Then when she addressed them in their native tongue, not in the French she had spoken since she was a toddler, they cheered until they were hoarse. John Knox, the fiery Protestant leader, was appalled, and he complained about "enchantment whereby men were bewitched".

Mary would have liked to restore the Catholic religion to the realm, but unlike her contemporary sovereigns, she was unwilling to use force. She was probably the only monarch of her era who never persecuted anyone for religious belief. Meanwhile, having her private chaplain, she practiced her own Faith.

She was realistic enough to know that the most she could hope for was to declare both religions legal—if indeed she could do that much without provoking Knox to lead a Protestant uprising. With this dual religion idea in view, she summoned Knox to her court and admonished him about inciting her subjects against her.

Futile words! Largely because of his demagoguery, Scotland remained a country divided by bitter antagonisms. Mary needed all her skill to govern and to keep the peace.

In her council were twelve members, seven Protestants, five Catholics. Furthermore, Scotland was not and never had been a united kingdom; it consisted of feudal estates, ruled by lairds who often warred among themselves.

Then Mary's problems were compounded by her Scottish Protestant half brother, James Stuart, earl of Moray. Since he was illegitimate (the son of her father by one of his mistresses), he could not reign, but he could and did make trouble at times by trying to thwart Mary's policies.

Mary's Guise uncles in France provided another complication: they reopened negotiations for the Spanish marriage. Although Mary had welcomed the match before, she now realized that to marry the Catholic Spanish prince would cause further unrest in Scotland, and it might debar her from ever succeeding to the throne of Protestant England. She had sent ambassadors to Elizabeth asking her to name her heir to the English throne.

Elizabeth was noncommittal. She feared to name Mary heir, for Mary's supporters both in Scotland and in England might then hurry Elizabeth to the grave via poison or dagger.

Meanwhile, Henry Stuart—Lord Darnley, an English-born and English-reared cousin of Elizabeth's and Mary's—traveled to Scotland. He was young, he was handsome, and Mary found him skilled in games and in playing the lute. She enjoyed his company and probably thought she was in love with him.

Soon the nobles were sanctioning a marriage of Mary to Darnley. Since Darnley was the great-grandson of Henry VII of England, the marriage would strengthen Mary's claim to the English throne.

But Darnley was a bit of a scoundrel; he was inordinately vain, he was a womanizer, and he was indolent, suspicious, and petty minded.

Still, Mary married him, and possibly she didn't notice his bad qualities in the beginning. Her hands were full with affairs of state. Aided and abetted by Queen Elizabeth, Mary's half brother, the ambitious Moray, was leading a rebellion against Mary. Mary rode out with her troops to quell it, galloping through a violent storm that uprooted trees. The men cheered her dauntless spirit. They loved and admired her (as did nearly everyone who came to know her well; her servants were fiercely loyal to her to the end).

The rebellion failed and Moray was temporarily imprisoned.

Shortly afterward Mary became pregnant. Though happy to have a child, Mary was disturbed because Darnley, her philandering husband, constantly nagged her to grant him the "Crown Matrimonial". She refused, because she did not trust his judgment enough to put additional power into his hands. But Darnley, being of a suspicious nature, suspected that Mary's Italian secretary, Riccio, had advised her to turn him down.

Some Protestant nobles hated Riccio too; they feared he might influence the queen to reinstate Catholicism in the realm. They suggested to Darnley that they might "remove" Riccio, and they promised that if Darnley would exonerate them from any act they might have to take to effect this "removal", they in turn would see that the queen gave him the "Crown Matrimonial".

He agreed, and one night when Mary was dining and Riccio was in the room, Darnley led the conspirators to her private apartments. Daggers in hand, they made for Riccio. "Fear not!" Mary cried, "The king will not suffer you to be killed." She stood before him with outstretched arms. A conspirator lunged at Riccio over her shoulder, and the victim's blood spattered on her gown. They then dragged Riccio away and inflicted fifty-six wounds, leaving the king's dagger in the corpse at last to show who had sanctioned the bloody deed.

Darnley and his cohorts then imprisoned Mary, and Darnley took it upon himself to dissolve Parliament so that its members could not mete out punishment to the assassins.

Mary knew that her one hope lay in placating Darnley, so instead of berating him when he visited her, she pointed out that he was imperiling the life of their unborn child, that she might suffer a miscarriage from the trauma of events. She also pointed out to him that men who were so disloyal to their anointed queen would be disloyal to him too; they would break promises they made to him. Then she warned him that her loyal subjects, once they learned he held her prisoner, would surely march against him.

Darnley was convinced. He unlocked the prison gates. Then he and Mary left the castle together and rode off to another of their strongholds.

Discovering Mary's escape, Darnley's allies fled to England. Darnley now denounced them and averred his own innocence. Few believed him.

Some months later, Mary's child was born, and she declared, "This is the prince whom I hope shall first unite the kingdoms of Scotland and England."

So he did! He later became James VI of Scotland and James I of England.

Among the most loyal and devoted nobles was the able, strong-willed earl of Bothwell. He was quite unlike either of Mary's boy husbands, and she was attracted to him. Certainly, she was unhappy with Darnley, and several nobles, including Bothwell, suggested that she seek an annulment on the grounds of her close relationship to Darnley. She refused, fearing an annulment might brand her son as illegitimate and so lose him the thrones of both Scotland and England. The nobles muttered about "some other way", and Mary, according to her enemies, was aware of this.

Meanwhile, Darnley fell ill while in his father's home. Mary brought him back to one of the royal castles. Did Mary, knowing that the nobles were planning to kill Darnley, wish to remove him from the protection of his father's stronghold?

It is an unanswerable question, and the so-called "casket letters" (probably forged) were supposed to show that Mary had plotted against Darnley with Bothwell.

At any rate, using gunpowder, the nobles blew up the castle when Darnley was within its walls and Mary was not. Darnley, attempting to escape, was caught and murdered.

Some accused Bothwell of the dark deed, although he was tried and found innocent by his peers. Then, when shortly afterward the earl abducted the queen, many believed that she connived in her own abduction.

Bothwell, who was married, managed to get an annulment, and Mary married her abductor. That she was much attracted to him seems clear. She quickly pardoned him legally for the abduction and created him duke of Orkney. She even bowed to his wishes and agreed (though it truly troubled her conscience) to a Protestant wedding—another evidence of her infatuation.

Soon a group of nobles, feigning righteous indignation at Darnley's murder, although some of them were party to it, attacked Bothwell in his castle. Mary was apprehended, and Bothwell was forced to flee to Denmark.

The queen's captors kept her imprisoned and demanded that she abdicate in favor of her infant son, James. Her half brother, Moray, was named regent.

But Mary had a weapon that her captors hadn't reckoned on—her charm. The laird of the castle where she was held, falling under her spell, placed few restrictions on her, so that Mary lived not only comfortably but enjoyed considerable freedom. Then his page became so enamored of Mary that he helped her escape. Disguised as a serving woman, she walked out of the castle.

Once free, her first act was to declare her abdication invalid because it was extorted under duress.

Thousands rallied to her side, but alas, enmity among them as well as the bungling of their leaders prevented Mary's forces, although they were twice the size of Moray's, from presenting a unified and strong front to Moray. When the inevitable battle came, it was a rout for Mary's troops.

Heartbreakingly, she had to flee. She went to England, seeking help from her sister sovereign and cousin, Elizabeth. Although during Mary's imprisonment Elizabeth had written promising "succour" and she had sent Mary a valuable ring in token of her good faith, Elizabeth did not welcome Mary. On the contrary, she, too, imprisoned Mary. Elizabeth reasoned that if Mary were free, she would be able to rally the Catholics of England to her cause, or if she went to France, the French might use Mary as an excuse to make trouble for England. In the castle where Mary was held, she had a few faithful attendants who had accompanied her from Scotland and she had a small income from France as dowager queen, but her life was made wretched by constant spying and by confinement. Furthermore, to her great distress, Elizabeth refused her a confessor throughout her long imprisonment—and even on the eve of her death.

The days crept by. Her followers in Scotland were defeated, one by one, although the castle of Edinburgh held out three long years. Several men lost their lives trying to rescue her from the English prison. Her son was taught to believe her a wicked woman, and he was persuaded to repudiate her publicly.

Mary wrote many letters, and her jailors had instructions

to allow her to smuggle some out so that Elizabeth could accuse her of plotting to escape and of plotting a Catholic insurrection.

It was only after nineteen long years that Mary was granted a court trail and it was granted then only to provide a semblance of legality for passing a death sentence. Mary was allowed no counsel, but she spoke eloquently in her own defense.

It was no use. The sentence was predetermined.

When it came, she accepted it calmly and unflinchingly. Her concern was to console her distraught and grieving attendants.

She was told that the reason she must die was that her existence threatened Protestantism in England. She answered, "I thank God and you for the honor you do me in regarding me as an instrument for the reestablishment of my religion in this Isle . . . and I will cheerfully shed my blood in that cause."

On the morning of her execution, she rose early, distributed her few possessions to her attendants, then knelt in prayer. All were weeping except Mary, who said, "You ought to rejoice and not weep . . . all the world is vanity. . . . Carry this message . . . to my friends that I died a true woman to my religion . . . a true Scottish woman and a true French woman."

She entered the execution chamber carrying a crucifix, and two Catholic Rosaries hung from her waist. With extraordinary composure, she walked across the great hall of Fotheringhay Castle and mounted the three steps to the execution platform.

A Protestant dean exhorted her to renounce her religion. She heard him out politely and then answered, "I am settled in the ancient, Catholic, Roman religion and mind to spend my blood in defense of it."

They stripped her of her remaining jewels. Then calmly she knelt and placed her head on the block. The axe was raised and she prayed, "Into thy hands I commend my spirit."

The axe fell, and her attendants noticed her little dog for the first time. Evidently, he had managed to creep into the hall, and now he stationed himself by her headless body and could not be coaxed nor driven away.

7

AMERICA'S PRIDE

Elizabeth Bayley Seton
(1774–1821)

It wasn't a cardinal or a bishop; it wasn't a priest or a monk; it was a widow with five children who pioneered the vast Catholic parochial school system of the United States. This woman, Elizabeth Bayley Seton, was the great innovator in Catholic education.

Moreover, it was this woman who established the Sisters of Charity in the United States, and since her day there have been thousands of these sisters who have cared for millions of people in schools, orphanages, and hospitals.

She was as American as Yankee Doodle. Her birth in 1774 almost coincided with the birth of our nation. It was exactly one week after she came into the world that the Continental Congress met in Philadelphia to protest against British rule. Typically American, too, was her inheritance of several different bloodlines—her ancestry was English, French, and Dutch.

Her childhood in her native city of New York was set against the backdrop of our War of Independence. Although her father, Dr. Richard Bayley, served during the war as a British Army surgeon, when the war ended he was happy to call himself American; by the time she was a young lady, he became chief health officer of the New York port. He was also the first professor of anatomy at one of America's oldest colleges, the college that was founded in colonial times as King's College and later patriotically renamed Columbia.

Although her family was affluent and socially prominent (connected to the Roosevelts, Barclays, DeLanceys, Pells, and DePeysters), this didn't make for a bright and carefree childhood. When she was a mere toddler, her mother died in giving birth to another child, and Betsy soon had a stepmother who, though she conscientiously tended the children of her husband's first marriage, did not show them much affection.

Nor was Betsy's father attentive to his children. His profession absorbed him, and he was rather indifferent to his family, going off to England for long periods at a time to study some new surgical technique and rarely bothering to write home.

Betsy was brought up to be a devout Episcopalian, and one thing she always thanked her stepmother for was a knowledge of the psalms. Religion was her strength during her childhood. Comfort came too from the very real affection between her and her sister, her half brothers and sisters, and other relatives. She enjoyed prolonged stays with an uncle and his family, where home life was warmed with love and laughter. Then she delighted in the gay parties and balls that came with her teens.

As she grew into a young lady, she and her father were closer than they had been before, and that, together with her meeting a charming young man, brought her happiness for the first time.

The young man was William Magee Seton, a descendent of one of Mary Queen of Scots' "four Mary's", that is, one of her ladies-in-waiting and dearest friends. William, or Willy as she called him, was the son of a well-to-do merchant importer-exporter, and since he was training for his father's business, William had spent several years abroad meeting business associates in London, Barcelona, Leghorn, Paris, and so on.

He and Betsy were married January 25, 1794, by the first bishop of the Protestant Episcopal Diocese of New York. Betsy was nineteen, Will twenty-five.

They were very much in love, so every day seemed just one more day of a honeymoon. Then too, Betsy was blessed in her new relatives. Her father-in-law, a jovial and generous man, made her feel most welcome and most wanted in his family of twelve now-motherless children. Betsy was particularly fond of her sister-in-law Rebecca and dubbed her "friend of my soul". Nor were there any money worries for Betsy and Will. They had a pleasant home on Wall Street, a few doors from the home of the Alexander Hamiltons. If anything else was needed to make Betsy say "My cup runneth over" it came when she found that she was pregnant. They named their firstborn, a girl, Anna Maria.

Grateful to God for her many blessings, the naturally pious and good-hearted Betsy worked with Rebecca and other young women in a group called the Widow's Society. They helped poor people, not by raising money for "the disadvantaged" but by visiting people and bringing them food and clothing—sometimes made by their own hands to fit the individual. Someone jokingly dubbed them "Protestant Sisters of Charity".

But in 1798 Betsy's Eden was disrupted. Her father-in-law became ill and died, much to the grief of his family and the many who dearly loved this generous, outgoing, kind man. His death may have been hastened by seeing his business suffer repeated, severe blows. In the English-French conflict, the Napoleonic War, the belligerents often seized ships and confiscated cargoes. Some Seton cargo-laden ships did not escape, and the loss was enormous.

The death of Will's father revolutionized Betsy's and Will's lives. They had to struggle not only with their grief and with financial worries but with an avalanche of other problems. The elder Mr. Seton left a large family—seven of them still at home. Since Will was the oldest, Betsy, only twenty-four herself, now felt she must act as a quasi-mother to them as well as to her own baby, Anna Maria, and she was expecting a second child.

Shortly after this second child was born, the business suffered what seemed the crowning blow: a ship with a particularly valuable cargo from Amsterdam was lost. Will, beside himself with worry, muttered about "poverty and prison".

He didn't go to prison, but the poverty was enough to force him to declare bankruptcy.

After that his health began to deteriorate, and when a second epidemic of yellow fever struck the city, Betsy worried continually, fearing he might fall victim.

He did not, but her father did. Conscientiously tending the ill night and day, he contracted the disease. His death, when it came, was a great sorrow to Betsy. During his latter years he had become close to her and to her children. (There were now three of them.) He was actually far more attentive and affectionate toward his grandchildren than he had been to his own children when they were young.

Sorrows, it seems, seldom come singly. Not many months later, Will was pronounced tubercular. Though terror stricken by this threat to his life, Betsy tried to appear as cheerful and calm as ever. Life went on, and she bore a fourth and fifth child.

Then as Will declined, his doctor prescribed the typical remedy of the era, "Rest and a sea voyage".

They decided to go to "sunny Italy" and visit old business friends, the two Filicchi brothers and their wives in Leghorn.

They could manage to take with them only their oldest, Anna. The other children they had to leave at home in the care of Rebecca.

They sailed from New York in October of 1803. The crossing was rough and stormy, and it took seven long weeks. Although Betsy wore a smiling face for Will's sake, she counted the days until the journey's end, but when it came, she was appalled to learn that they were forbidden to go inland to their friends' home. The Italian authorities, fearing the yellow fever contagion of New York, quarantined the Setons in the Lazaretto, a bleak, cold, stone building.

They held them there over a month, and it was during the rainy season. Each hour, each moment seemed an eternity, as Will lay there white and shivering and coughing blood. Betsy wrote in her journal of her husband "who left his all to seek a milder climate, confined to this place of high and damped walls; exposed to cold and wind which penetrates the very bones; without fire except the kitchen charcoal."

Before Betsy's horrified eyes, he grew rapidly weaker and thinner and paler, but she could do nothing. His friends, the Filicchis, sent nourishing food and a servant to wait on him, but that, helpful though it was in some ways, could not halt the progress of Will's disease. Betsy prayed more ardently than she ever had in her life. Little Anna jumped rope to keep warm or studied the Bible lessons that her mother assigned her.

By the time they were finally released, Betsy knew the worst was at hand. Two days after Christmas and less than three months after they had left home, Will died. Betsy was to say later, "It seemed that I loved him more than any one could love on earth."

Stunned, stranded, and sorrowing, she turned to the Filicchis. The greatest comfort they could offer was assurance of their faith in God and in eternal life. Although Betsy had faith herself, somehow their faith seemed a firmer rock than her own. She asked them about their Catholicism, and since she was detained in Italy by Anna's contracting scarlet fever, the questions were numerous. Also in that atmosphere she seemed to soak up Catholicism through her very pores.

At last she was able to go home to her younger children; she hugged them as though she would never let them go.

Then new sorrow! Her "friend of my soul", her sister-in-law Rebecca, became ill and died about a month after her arrival.

The grieving Betsy again turned to religion. Formerly it had offered some sure comfort, but now, like an uninvited guest, the thought of Catholicism kept invading her prayers and with it came the question: "Does God want me to abandon the Anglican church that has always been home to me?"

At Mr. Filicchi's suggestion, she wrote to the Catholic bishop Carroll. He answered, "Seek and ye shall find." Since that was exactly what she thought she had been doing, his advice did not help either.

Now she was tempted to say, "A plague on both your houses." Certainly *she* couldn't decide between the two religions. Only God could! So she prayed for guidance, using the quotation, "If I am right, O teach my heart still in the right to stay; if I am wrong, thy grace impart to find the better way."

After a long, painful period and after instructions from a Fr. de Cheverus, she felt that the Lord had made the answer clear. On Ash Wednesday, March 14, 1805, she was received into the Church at St. Peter's Catholic Church, New York City.

A storm broke! Friends and relatives were shocked. They

wept, threatened, and scolded. In the beginning, New York
had been a Protestant colony and, as everyone pointed out,
the Catholics who had arrived since the War of Independence were both ignorant and oafish. How could she identify
with them?

She couldn't argue, so she tried to keep calm and to direct
her thoughts to plans for the future. She had little money
and five dependent children. Her affluent paternal relatives,
who would ordinarily have insisted on helping her, now felt
that she had put herself beyond the pale, that she had
indicated she did not want their way of life or them.

Clearly, her priority must be to find paying work. She had
some competence in teaching. She had not sent her children
to school in the primary grades but instead had set aside
certain hours of each day to teach them writing, reading,
grammar, arithmetic, French, and Bible stories. Some of her
friends' children had joined her classes, so in effect she had
run a miniature school. Moreover, she was well educated,
well read, and she spoke French fluently.

She now worked out an agreement with an English
Catholic gentleman named White to teach in a boys' school
he was opening. All looked rosy until someone circulated
the report that these Catholics had gotten together to
proselytize the students, and there was a loud outcry, so the
school had to close its doors.

Her next venture, a boardinghouse for students, netted
insufficient funds to cover all her expenses.

About this time, her sister-in-law Cecilia became a
Catholic, and the Seton family not only blamed Betsy for
"corrupting" the girl, they threatened to run Betsy out of
town.

She considered teaching in Canada, until she met a Father
Dubourg, S.S., from Baltimore, who proposed, "Why not

open a girls' academy in Maryland? People there will welcome your religiously oriented instruction."

Maryland, founded by Catholics under Lord Baltimore, was as Catholic as New York was Protestant, so Betsy was well received there. A former governor of the state, Colonel John Eager Howard (by blood of the English nobility), even offered her, though she declined it, a home in his mansion, and many other people gave her encouragement and help.

Guided by priests, she opened a small school next door to St. Mary's Seminary, which aimed, her biographer explains, "to teach the science of the world in the light of eternity".

She had the dedication of a nun, and her life of teaching, prayer, meditation, and austerity was indistinguishable from that of a professed religious. Indeed, she resolved that as soon as it was practicable she would actually take the classic religious vows of poverty, chastity, and obedience.

Her priest mentors, Fathers Dubourg, de Cheverus, Babade, and others, recommended to her young women of refinement and education who had similar ideas, and they soon joined her, helped in the teaching, and adopted her routine. They adopted, too, a "habit", which was similar to the "widow's weeds" that Betsy (now always titled more formally, either Elizabeth or Mrs. Seton) was wearing. They called themselves "sisters".

Planters and businessmen were happy to send their daughters to these gentlewomen to learn not only the three R's, but religion, gracious manners, and "deportment".

Enrollment so increased that Elizabeth soon outgrew the school building. But "the Lord provides", and Samuel Cooper, a seminarian of considerable means who attended St. Mary's Seminary, offered to finance a new school for "the advancement of Catholic female children in habits of religion".

He purchased land west of Baltimore near the town of Emmitsburg. The site was chosen because it was near St.

Mary's boys' school run by the Sulpician Fathers, the same
Order that ran the seminary in Baltimore. These priests
could act as chaplains and advisers for the sisters. Elizabeth
was delighted too that she could now enroll her two boys
in St. Mary's, where she would have them close by.

The little group of women lived in great simplicity and,
during the first year especially, with some hardship.

But the school did well, and the tuition plus an occasional
donation from the ever-loyal Filicchis and from some
wealthy parents of pupils kept things going. Then, more
surprising, in a few years, nearly every one of Elizabeth's
family and friends who had been so hostile to Catholicism
did an about face, and some began to help her financially.

In many ways Elizabeth ran the school as she had run her
home. Moral training was intertwined with scholastic
teaching. A traditional punishment in the home had been
standing a child in the corner. Now, using a variation of
that, she had an erring child kneel or sit before Christ's
picture and think of her fault. Once a pupil, the granddaugh-
ter of Charles Carroll of Carrollton and daughter of General
Harper, the famous lawyer, orator, congressman, and
senator, asked a schoolmate, "Do you know who I am? My
father is General Robert Goodloe Harper!" Within minutes
Elizabeth had the child sitting before the picture of Christ
reflecting that she was important only for the same reason
that everyone was important: Christ had died for her.

Elizabeth and Mr. Cooper discussed dreams of a school,
novel for that era, that would not only make religious and
moral training a priority but that would admit both boys
and girls, including children whose parents could not afford
the tuition at the academy. Such a school would run, as did
Elizabeth's, with the approval and cooperation of the parish
priest rather than under the jurisdiction of the head of some
religious Order. Elizabeth had the vision to see the future

need for such a school and to begin working and planning toward it.

It was actually Bishop Neumann of a later date who systematized the parochial school network as we know it today. But as Elizabeth's biographer, Joseph I. Dirvin, C.M., said, "No jumble of technicalities and definitions can obscure the fact that St. Joseph's Academy was the archetype of American Catholic elementary education."

A prime move to implement her ideas was her original desideratum, that she and her fellow teachers take religious vows. She hoped to affiliate with the Sisters of Charity in France, so the bishop asked that three sisters from a French convent come to Emmitsburg to train the sisters there in the spirit of the Order.

Meantime, he obtained a copy of the Rules for Elizabeth, but there were difficulties in arranging for sisters to come from France, which may have been providential, for the American group had ideas that might not have dovetailed exactly with those of the sisters from across the sea. There were questions as to how much, if any, they should put themselves under the jurisdiction of the superiors of the French Order.

The group's first move was to elect Elizabeth Superior (against her will), and they began to call her Mother Seton. In 1812 she took her vows before Bishop Carroll. After a year's probation, eighteen other sisters (among them Mother Seton's two sisters-in-law, Harriet and Cecilia Seton, who had become Catholics and joined Mother Seton in Emittsburg) took their vows. Shortly afterward Mother Seton opened a novitiate for ten candidates.

The women followed the Rule of the French Sisters of Charity but with a few distinctly American twists, so that they formed in effect a new Order—the first independent religious Order in the United States—and the state of

Maryland granted incorporation under the title "The Sisters of Charity of St. Joseph".

One point Mother Seton had insisted upon in the new Rule was latitude to fulfill freely her obligation to her children. She said, "By the law of the Church I so much love, I could never take an obligation that interfered with my duties to them."

Elizabeth took full advantage of these clauses, especially when her daughter Anna fell ill. But despite her tender care, Anna did not recover. Before she died, the girl, only sixteen, begged to be allowed—and was allowed—to take her vows and become one of the religious community. That was a consolation to the grieving Elizabeth.

Anna was the first sister to join the original group of American Sisters of Charity. Many came later, and although during her lifetime Elizabeth did not open another school, she was able to send, at the request of bishops, sisters to found orphanages in Philadelphia and in New York. The Philadelphia institution was the first Catholic American orphanage.

Since schools were her priority, Elizabeth continued to plan for future possibly parish-connected schools and began a Training School for Teachers at Emmitsburg. Elizabeth stressed (as parochial schools still ideally do today) not only scholastic education in no-nonsense, basic subjects but also respect for legitimate authority and, above all, moral training and doctrinal instruction.

About this time she had the first intimation that she, like her dear Willy, had contracted tuberculosis. One wonders how much attention she paid to the symptoms at first; she was so busy as the mother of five children, as the Mother Superior of a group of women, and as principal of a school. Then in her "spare" time she managed to translate from

French to English several books, including a biography of St. Vincent de Paul and of Mlle. Le Gras.

Moreover, she had much on her mind and heart; her youngest child became ill and died as had Anna, and her two sons, now grown, moved away. She sorely missed them, and she once wrote to son William, a naval officer, "The hardest penance I can pay in this life is separation from you."

By 1818 Elizabeth's life had entered the final stage. From then on her strength visibly ebbed, and on January 4, 1821, when she was forty-seven years old, death came to claim her.

Her work did not die with her. Her sisters in religion carried on. Soon they established schools in Baltimore, Cincinnati, and other places.

During a meeting of the American hierarchy in 1852, Archbishop Kendrick of Baltimore declared, "Elizabeth Seton did more for the Church in America than all of us bishops together." She had opened the first Catholic parish school and had set the pattern for future such schools; she founded the first American religious community and had opened the first Catholic orphanage in the United States.

In 1880 Cardinal Gibbons of Baltimore (then archbishop) urged that steps be taken toward her canonization.

On September 14, 1975, in St. Peter's of Rome, Pope Paul VI declared this woman, Elizabeth Anne Bayley Seton, to be a saint.

She is remembered, then, not only for being among America's great educators—possibly its single most influential and most innovative—but for being the first native-born American citizen, man or woman, to attain canonization.

8

THE LADY OF THE LAMP

Florence Nightingale

(1820–1910)

Say "Florence Nightingale", and instantly the word *nurse* pairs with it. Probably she was the most extraordinary nurse in history. Kings, queens, and princes all consulted her, as did the president of the United States, who wanted her advice about military hospitals during the Civil War. She did so much for humanity that she was every nation's heroine. Award after award fell into her lap, but she shrank from the limelight and even left instructions that at her death there was to be no national funeral nor burial in Westminster Abbey.

It was Florence Nightingale who revolutionized hospital methods in England—and indeed throughout the world. During the Crimean War, she served in the first field hospital ever run and tended by women. She established schools for training nurses, and she introduced procedures that have been benefiting mankind ever since. She also wrote reference books to guide future generations.

Still, this is an incomplete portrait; for years Florence acted as behind-the-scenes British secretary of war, managing to change drastically, and to better considerably, conditions for men in the armed services by setting up a health administration system sans precedent. Moreover, she reversed the British government's policy toward India. She was sure that nothing could be done to bring justice, law, or freedom to

India until the people had enough to eat. She insisted that agricultural development, which depended on irrigation, be the priority.

Suffering, wherever it existed, challenged her. She even set up a system for extending nursing care to the poor and the criminal underworld in the slums of English cities.

One reason Florence managed to accomplish so much was because she was what we call today a "workaholic"; she took no rest nor recreation, as most people define such things. Or rather, her work *was* her rest and her recreation. Any occupation but working for improved health standards seemed to her a waste of time. And she had remarkable stamina; when she was young, she sometimes worked twenty-two hours of the twenty-four. Then too, she was gifted with a peculiar genius: she could assimilate information in prodigious quantities, retain it, marshal her facts, and use them effectively.

One of her associates, a Dr. Farr, said that Florence found statistics "more enlivening than a novel". This was because she saw people behind the dry pellets of information— individual people with faces that showed suffering or people who had some pressing need that she might be able to meet. When the doctor told her, "I have a New Year's gift for you. It is in the shape of tables of figures", she answered, "I am exceedingly anxious to see your charming gift especially the figures about deaths, admissions and diseases", and she really meant "charming". A relative wrote that when Flo was exhausted, the sight of a column of figures was "perfectly reviving to her".

Inferences that she drew from facts crammed her books and her reports. Altogether she wrote eight lengthy reports and seventeen books on medical and nursing subjects, if one counts her published *Indian Letters* and her published addresses to probationer nurses in the "Nightingale Fund School".

Florence was born in 1820 while her English parents, Fanny and William, were vacationing in Florence, Italy. She was named for her birthplace, although at that time Florence was not listed among feminine names, as it has been since Miss Nightingale gave it fame. She had an older sister Parthenope (always called Parthe), who was also named for her birthplace.

Florence's beautiful and intelligent mother and her wealthy dilettante father were not very compatible, nor were the two little girls. Parthe, though she all but adored her sister "Flo", at the same time was envious and selfishly possessive of her. From birth, Flo had seemed exceptional; for one thing she was highly intelligent and passionately intense, and so she was the natural leader, and Parthe, who was less intelligent, less intense, less pretty, and certainly less exceptional, came to depend on Flo for everything— and to resent it.

Because it was impossible to find a tutor with the intellectual prowess demanded by Mr. Nightingale, he himself taught the children Latin, Greek, German, Italian, French, English grammar, philosophy, and history, while a governess was trusted to teach them only music and drawing. Their regimen meant unremitting study. For Parthe, study was struggle and hardship; for Flo it was a priceless opportunity to learn concentration and industry.

When Parthe was eighteen and Flo sixteen, study was somewhat curtailed. The girls were presented at court and introduced to society; their life then included many parties and much travel on the Continent. Flo was tall, willowy, graceful, and pretty, while Parthe was rather plain looking. Everywhere Flo shone, and she enjoyed being admired and sought after. Two young men promptly fell in love with her and proposed marriage. She like them both, but she wasn't ready to marry either. Meanwhile, she certainly enjoyed dancing with them; she was an excellent and avid dancer.

Then a strange thing happened. Though she did not think herself deeply religious and never thought she became so, on February 7, 1837, when she was scarcely seventeen years old, she felt that God spoke to her, calling her to future "service". From that time on her life was changed.

At first the call disturbed her. Not knowing the nature of the "service", she feared making herself unworthy of whatever it was by leading the frivolous life that her mother and her social set demanded of her. Now she was given to periods of preoccupation, or to what she called "dreams" of how to fulfill her mission. Meanwhile, she spent all extra and odd moments visiting the cottages on her family estate and bringing neighboring poor people food and medicine. Then when a family friend died in childbirth, Flo begged her parents to let her stay at the country home year round and take care of the baby instead of going to London for the winter social season. They vetoed the idea, believing she should mingle in society, eventually choose a husband, and bear children of the family bloodline. Then too, Parthe had hysterics at the very thought of the "ungrateful and unfeeling Flo" wanting to be separated from her.

In London one of Flo's suitors again pressed her for an answer to his marriage proposal. She liked him, but she could not bring herself to say yes, especially when she did not know what "service" lay ahead. Visiting her family home at the time were Dr. Howe and his wife Julia Ward Howe (author of the "Battle Hymn of the Republic"). She asked Dr. Howe, "Do you think it unsuitable and unbecoming for a young Englishwoman to devote herself to works of charity in hospitals and elsewhere as Catholic sisters do? Do you think it would be a dreadful thing?"

He answered that it would be unusual and "whatever is unusual in England is thought unsuitable", but nonetheless he advised her, "Act on your inspiration."

If she were to consider nursing her "service", (and she was beginning to believe it must be), then she knew that she needed training. She proposed going to an infirmary run by a family friend. Her parents were shocked, horrified, angry! She was a gentlewoman! Parthe meanwhile had her usual hysterics and accused Flo of being in love with "some low, vulgar surgeon".

Their objections were understandable. In that era, English hospitals were places of degradation and filth. The malodorous "hospital smell" was literally nauseating to many, and nurses usually drank heavily to dull their senses. Flo herself admitted that the head nurse of a London hospital told her that "in the course of her long experience she had never known a nurse who was not drunken, and there was immoral conduct in the very wards."

But at least Flo could study on her own. From a friend in Parliament, Sidney Herbert, she procured government reports on national health conditions, then she got up in the dark of predawn every morning and pored over them by the light of an oil lamp, filling notebook after notebook with facts and figures, which she indexed and tabulated.

Since she had an unusually retentive memory, she soon had detailed information at her fingertips. Still, she lacked practical experience. She planned to acquire that by going to the unquestionably moral Institution of Lutheran Deaconesses in Kaiserwerth, Germany. Although her father called the move "theatrical", and although Parthe again had hysterics, her parents reluctantly allowed her to go.

After the Kaiserwerth stint she wrote that she felt "as if

nothing could ever vex me again", but soon the old pattern reappeared: her parents wanted her to lead a "normal" life and were baffled and annoyed when she turned down another eligible suitor and seemed indifferent to marriage; Parthe as usual could not make a move without "dear sister".

Then Florence met and confided in Cardinal Manning. He understood her aims, and she wondered if Catholicism could be her gateway to "service". She proposed becoming a Catholic, but the cardinal demurred because she rejected certain Catholic tenets. However, he arranged for her to enter a Paris hospital staffed by nuns who obviously didn't resort to drink. She would wear the postulant habit, but she would live apart from the nuns.

Once in Paris, she took time to go first to every hospital in the city to see various nursing methods. Then shortly after she arrived at the hospital where she was to serve, ironically enough, she came down with measles and had to leave.

By happy chance another door opened. Back in England, the Institution for Care of Sick Gentlewomen in Distressed Circumstances needed a superintendent. Florence's study of health, hospital problems, and management recommended her. While she held this job, she began visiting English and Scotch hospitals to collect data to establish a case for bettering conditions elsewhere. When cholera broke out and nurses, fearing the disease, refused to serve, Florence acted as a nurse herself and earned universal respect.

Then the Crimean War erupted. English military hospitals were a disgrace; in them a wounded man had almost no chance of recovery. When a reporter wrote that the French took far better care of their wounded, English consciences were stung into action. Florence's friend Sidney Herbert, now secretary of war, not only authorized purchase of hospital equipment but created a new official position to

which he appointed the best-qualified person he knew,
Florence Nightingale. She became "Superintendent of the
Female Nursing Establishment of the English General
Hospitals in Turkey", and she was to go to Crimea, taking
nurses of her choice. Her authority was to be plenary and
absolute.

Previously, no woman had even entered a military
hospital, but because of Miss Nightingale's reputation (she
was called Miss Nightingale by the public), the order was
applauded.

Now to implement it! First, how was she to find good
nurses? Through Cardinal Manning a great concession was
made, and ten Catholic sisters were allowed to go to Turkey
under Miss Nightingale's leadership, subject to her orders.
Eight Anglican sisters joined too, and Florence painstakingly
gathered other women.

On arrival, they found moldy food, scarce water, filth,
overcrowding, no sanitary arrangements, no bedsheets, no
operating tables, no medical supplies. The forty nurses were
allotted a kitchen and five rat-and-vermin-infested bed-
rooms; this meant crowding many nurses into one room
while Florence and one companion slept in a closet.

Miss Nightingale had authority to requisition supplies, so
she quickly asked for towels and soap and insisted that
clothes be washed and floors scrubbed. Then she ran into
trouble; some officers and doctors grumbled about her
power. After that she tried to make it seem that suggestions
came from them and that she was just their agent. That
helped only a little, and fresh difficulties arose.

Maddening red tape hindered her at every turn. Then the
Superior of the Catholic sisters, although she had agreed to
accept Miss Nightingale's leadership, questioned why
anyone but herself should direct the sisters, and she
constantly made trouble. The Anglican nuns felt that

Florence favored the Catholics. Only the patients, the wounded men, fully approved of her, and they all but adored the "Lady with the Lamp", as they called her when she visited the wards at the end of the day. They spoke of "kissing her very shadow" as she passed.

Despite difficulties, Miss Nightingale went on working. She dressed wounds, administered or supervised medical treatments, instructed nurses, made rounds of the wards, and then, before she dropped exhausted into bed near midnight, she spent an hour or two writing reports for the government at home. She also suggested legislation to help the men; for example, the old law mandated that hospitalized men, since they were no longer in danger of being shot, have their pay cut. But their wounds often handicapped them for life, so Miss Nightingale opposed the pay cuts and wrote directly to Queen Victoria to explain why. The men's pay was restored.

This was just one instance among many where she suggested or wrote legislation that her friend Sidney Herbert introduced in Parliament. Deploring the fact that the soldiers, when not in combat, spent so much time drinking, she wrote a bill authorizing appropriations for a room with daily papers, books, games, magazines, writing paper, and so on and arranged for the bill's passage through the usual channels. Unremarkable as such a bill may seem today, it was remarkable then, and some officers complained that she was coddling the men. Again, too, they resented her power. By changing conditions for the army, she was, they said, acting as secretary of war. She was responsible even for a bill that allowed illiterate soldiers to learn to read and write at government expense.

Still, some doctors and officers respected and admired her efficiency and her dedication, and the English public as well as troops idolized her. When the war ended, she was the sole hero to emerge. As one biographer said, "She had the country at her feet." The queen presented Florence with a diamond brooch inscribed on the reverse side "To Miss Florence Nightingale as a mark of esteem and gratitude for her devotion towards the Queen's brave soldiers from Victoria R. 1855." The troops set up "The Nightingale Fund" in her honor and contributed a huge sum. Eventually she used it for a nurses' training school.

Now she needed a rest. In Crimea she had collapsed once or twice from overwork, and she returned home gaunt, pale, and suffering from several ailments. But she had no intention of resting. Military reforms were urgently needed. The mortality rate (73 percent in six months from diseases alone) was outrageous, and it resulted not from battlefield casualties but from the execrable system of the British army's health administration. She wanted to push reform while the public was still indignant enough to be supportive. But she was afraid that given the jealousy of the officers, any reform linked to her name would die aborning. She went into seclusion while she wrestled with the problem.

Her aims were furthered when the queen summoned her to palace visits (and indeed the queen even amazingly dropped in on her informally in her home). The women became friends, and Florence convinced Victoria of the value of her reforms. Although royalty could not act directly, the queen summoned the secretary of state to the palace along with Florence, so that she had an opportunity to present her ideas to him and to try to persuade him to act.

He hemmed and hawed; he really didn't want to bother. But Florence kept at him until he at least appointed a commission to study the matter. He then asked her for a detailed report. Night and day, she worked on the report; it ran 1,000 pages. She worked with the commission members, who called her "commander in chief". She collected facts, collated and verified them, then she coached the men who were her mouthpieces, feeding them the conclusions she drew from those facts.

All this had a price tag: she became ill. Still, she went on working. To gain public support, she wrote articles illustrated by her charts. Then she collapsed. She was seriously ill, but she had won her point! The government acted.

A friend, Sir John McNeill, wrote her, "To you more than to any other man or woman alive will henceforth be due the welfare and efficiency of the British army. I thank God that I have lived to see your success."

When her health improved, people came to her for advice, among them the queen of Holland and the crown prince of Prussia. Between visitors, she wrote books. *Notes on Hospitals,* specifying needs and arrangements for an efficient hospital, ran into three editions and was widely translated into other languages. After its publication, the king of Portugal asked her to design a hospital in Lisbon, and the government of India consulted her about a hospital in Madras. Her next book, *Notes on Nursing,* sold thousands of copies in factories, villages, and schools and was translated into French, German, and Italian.

Writing mostly at night and working by day, she opened a nurses' training school, using the money given by the troops to the Nightingale Fund. Her standards were very high; she demanded the best. If she had not done so before, surely now she changed forever the image of a nurse from that of a "drunken hussy" to that of an efficient attendant of the ill.

All was going well for her except that she deeply grieved for the death of two dear friends, Sidney Herbert and Arthur Clough; both had helped her push through health legislation. Although Miss Nightingale loved humanity, she did not love it to the exclusion of individual humans; she really loved these men—platonically. Her grief, together with her grueling schedule, made her ill again, but not so ill that she could not initiate another reform move. It involved no less than the reorganization of the War Office. One of her friends said that she was virtually secretary of state in the War Office for the next five years.

During her "tenure", she wanted to guide the Sanitary Commission on the Health of the Army in India. Again she plunged into facts and figures and made herself an authority on Indian conditions, so much so that the viceroy to India consulted her and through him she was able to effect some reforms.

Her next big task came when a prominent Liverpool philanthropist approached her, begging nursing care for slum dwellers and workhouse inmates. She arranged to supply the care; moreover, she called for legislation that would provide separate facilities for the children, the insane, and the victims of communicable diseases, who had previously lived cheek by jowl in the same workhouses.

No letup followed. Next came the Franco-Prussian War, during which she worked with the National Society for Aid to the Sick and Wounded, later called the British Red Cross Aid Society. When the war ended, Jean Henri Dunant said, "Though I'm known as the founder of the Red Cross . . . it is to an Englishwoman that all the honor . . . is due. What inspired me . . . was the work of Florence Nightingale."

For an interval, however, she did slacken her public work to devote herself to nursing first her dying father, then her dying mother, and then her dying sister, Parthe, with whom she was closer than in bygone years.

She lived on into old age, always supervising work at the Nightingale Fund School and always and everywhere being treated with a respect akin to awe. In 1907 Edward VII bestowed on her the Order of Merit; it was the first time it had ever been given to a woman. Ministers, kings, and princes as well as the children of the nurses she trained frequently called to see her and to consult her. Parthe's widower husband called on her every day. She continued to write until her sight failed, her memory dulled, and she became a little vague.

Death, when due, came gently. On August 13, 1910, she fell asleep around noon and did not awaken.

9

WOMAN WITH A WIDE MISSION

Frances Cabrini

(1850–1917)

A golden statue stands in the temple of Soochow, China, to honor the fourteenth-century Italian traveler Marco Polo. Far more than a golden statue stands in many cities of the Western world to honor the nineteenth-century Italian traveler Frances Cabrini. Wherever she went, there arose orphanages, schools, hospitals, and settlement houses. The indefatigable, diminutive, and dynamic woman traveler, though primarily a missionary, was also a builder, an executive, and an innovator. To accomplish her feats, she crossed the Atlantic thirty times in an era sans commercial planes, and she traveled through much of North, Central, and South America in a era when the few trains that existed were comparatively primitive.

From the time that she was a little girl in her native Lombardian village of Sant' Angelo (near Lodi and about twenty miles from Milan), she dreamed of telling other children who did not know Jesus all about how good he was and how much he did for them. On a creek near her home, she would sail toy boats filled with violets and play the age-old "let's pretend" game, saying to herself, "The violets are my friends and I. We're going to far-off lands as missionaries."

When she grew older, thinking that the techniques for giving religious instruction would be similar to techniques for giving instruction in other subjects, she trained to be a teacher. But once graduated, her envisioned life's work seemed "the impossible dream". She had always been considered frail and delicate, and the members of her large and loving family—she was the "baby" of thirteen children—insisted that she couldn't stand the rigors of missionary life. "Besides," they argued, "There aren't any women missionaries. That kind of work is for men."

The girl definitely had determination; she set her jaw firmly and resolved that she would find a way. Meanwhile, she did some substitute teaching, but once out of the classroom, her mind, like a released spring, snapped back to the old groove and she tried to figure out how to become a missionary.

Alas, she could find no missionary Order for women. Apparently, her family was right when they told her "Only men do missionary work."

With a sigh, she decided that she could at least enter a teaching Order and teach Christian children their cate-chism, but the Superior of a nearby convent shook her head and said, "You're too frail for the strenuous life that a religious must lead."

What next? There was no use sitting in a corner and wringing her hands. A priest asked her to take charge of an orphanage, where she was allowed to be on the periphery of a religious community. The job was strenuous, but she averred that her health improved with hard work. All the while, though, she kept thinking about those "far-off missions". Later, she was to write that, if possible, "I'd build a steamer and call it Christopher—bearer of Christ—and I would travel . . . to make known the name of Christ." A priest in whom she confided challenged, "Why not found your own religious Order?"

Her eyes lit up as though a switch had been thrown. A

heaven-inspired idea! With God's help, she'd do it! What matter that there had never been an Order of women expressly dedicated to missionary work? There had to be a first for everything.

How she attracted other girls who were willing to travel to China or to any other place to bring word of Christ, how she procured diocesan funds, and all the rest is a tale in itself. Suffice it to say, she did manage to do all this, but she had to begin her project by opening, in the town of Codogno, a novitiate to train young sisters in missionary work.

Then she had to—and she wanted to—seek papal approval to make her Order official. In 1887 she and six other girls went to Rome for that purpose. The Pope was encouraging and supportive of this new Order, which Frances called the Institute of the Missionary Sisters of the Sacred Heart, but he told her, "Go to the west, not the east."

He explained that the 50,000 Italian immigrants in New York City were lost "babes in the wood". They were confused and ill at ease. First of all, when they attended American churches, they were not really welcomed, and being ignorant of English, they did not feel at home in these churches anyway. They drifted away from religion, and their children grew up never hearing of Christ.

The Pope's westward directive amounted to a command, so Frances made an about face and looked to America.

Before she and her sisters left their native land in 1889, the supposedly "frail" girl saw a doctor. He said baldly, "You probably have only about two more years to live but you might as well live those years overseas as here, if that's what you want."

An Italian countess had offered to finance an orphanage for children of Italian immigrants in New York City. However, when the sisters arrived there and called on the archbishop, he declared another orphanage in New York to be "superfluous"; nor would he allow one in the section that they had chosen. He said he would give them permission to open a shelter in the Italian Quarter, but he added, "Your best move is to return to Italy."

The sisters, and indeed Mother Cabrini too (as she was now called), turned deathly pale, but Mother, having a commission from the Pope, answered boldly if quietly in her heavily accented English, "No, your Grace, that is impossible. I have been sent here by the Holy See, and here I will stay."

Within four short months, Mother Cabrini gathered together 400 poor Italian children of the New York slums, whom she cared for spiritually, intellectually, and physically. The physical care took some doing because money was always scarce. The archbishop (having been won over by seeing Mother at work) supplied some funds, the countess helped, a few poor Italian immigrants threw in an occasional widow's mite, but still it was not easy. That the sisters succeeded so well in caring for the children was a near miracle, because it was like feeding pigeons: one was never done since more kept coming.

Supplying their religious education, though primary, wasn't quite enough. Italian immigrant children were not attending the English-speaking American schools, so they were growing up without any secular education except what they picked up on the streets. Mother found an abandoned old house that she used as a school for them and saw that they received an elementary secular education along with their religious instruction.

Now all of this created, within just months after Mother's arrival in the United States, a desperate need for more sisters to help with the teaching, the bookkeeping, the cooking, the washing, the counseling, and all the rest. Although a few Irish immigrants asked to join the Order and were accepted with open arms, Mother realized that they could not substitute for Italian sisters who understood the language and the temperament of their charges. To recruit Italian sisters, she made the first of her many trips back to Italy and to the novitiate she had founded. Seven young sisters joined her on the return trip to America.

Then heaven sent her a lagniappe. The Jesuits owned, in West Park on the Hudson, a large building set in spacious grounds that they called Manresa; this they sold Mother, with all its furnishings, for a song. They warned of a water shortage on the place, but a quickly dug well corrected the shortage. Soon the building held 300 orphans from New York City. The city house then became the recruiting station where children were received before then went to Manresa.

Concurrently, the New York City school was growing. By this time it had about 250 pupils. And there were a larger number of children in Sunday schools in those parishes where the sisters taught every Sunday morning. So still more sisters were needed, and again Mother set out for Italy.

While there, Pope Leo XIII gave her some Church funds, and obeying an ecclesiastical directive, she opened a residence for students of a normal school in Rome. Its purpose was to surround young girls with a wholesome atmosphere to help safeguard their morals. Since most of the girls were poor, Mother wanted to offer many of them free board, and she declared, "I will turn all Rome upside down but I will have twenty free places next year."

She certainly didn't have to go that far, for within a month a second Roman countess stepped forward and saw that Mother had money to supply the twenty free places.

She was now ready to return to New York. This time she took with her twenty-eight sisters. She almost didn't make it because of a violent storm on the high seas, the worst in

many years. Several ships ran into trouble that night, but
not hers.

She and her sisters had scarcely landed in New York when
a Nicaraguan woman wrote that she had gathered together,
and was caring for, a group of orphans. She and the bishop
of her country begged Mother Cabrini to come to Nicaragua
and start a school.

Mother consulted Rome, and the answer was "Go". As
soon as she could raise money for passage, she and fourteen
of the twenty-eight sisters who had just come from Italy
were on their way.

Like all the institutions that Mother set up, the Nicaraguan
school flourished, so that in fairly short order, she was able
to leave it with trusted lieutenants and return to the United
States. This time she went to New Orleans, where a group
of Italian immigrants, like those in New York, were having
troubles. Some had commited crimes, and after a policeman
was killed, eleven Sicilians were accused of murder. The
Sicilians were acquitted in court, but an angry mob, still
believing them guilty, broke into the jail and hanged the
unfortunate men.

The local archbishop had begged Mother to open a
settlement house in his diocese. She complied, and in two
months had three sisters there.

When things were beginning to run fairly smoothly, an
Italian bishop in New York pleaded with Mother to return
to New York and staff a hospital there with her sisters.

The request made her furrow her brow in perplexity. She
wanted her Order to bring help to souls; care of bodies,
though important, was secondary. But should she refuse the
bishop?

"Lord, direct me", she prayed. Then one night she dreamed
that she saw the Madonna going from bed to bed in a hospital

tending the ill. When Mother questioned her, the Madonna said, "Frances, I'm doing what you refuse to do."

After that, Mother sent ten of her sisters to the hospital. But an inefficient hospital manager had run the place hopelessly into debt, and soon the property had to be liquidated.

Was the nursing an exercise in futility? Was Mother's first reaction correct, that her Order shouldn't tackle hospital work?

Mother did not reason that way. The dream still seemed authentic. Besides, she actually felt that the hospital experience had been valuable: it had proved that hospital work was, after all, as important as the work she had been doing, for it too provided opportunities to help people spiritually as well as physically. It did not take her long, then, to go on to the next step: she should start her own hospital. She paid a month's rent on a large building, bought ten beds for the patients as a start (the sisters at first were to sleep on the floor), and laid her plans for the future opening of what she called "Columbus Hospital". The Italians, religious or irreligious, were delighted with the name. Columbus was their hero!

But before Columbus Hospital's doors opened, the perennial need for more sisters was obvious, so again it was back to Italy and to the novitiate to recruit them. (Incidentally, while Mother was in Italy, the Pope gave her generous monetary help, and he told her, "Heaven is made for those who work like you do.")

In due time, Columbus Hospital was functioning, and in the black. As a biographer said of Mother, "She had a genius for using funds advantageously." Shortly afterward, New York State granted formal approbation and legal incorporation.

Throughout Mother Cabrini's life, hospitals, orphanages, schools, and other institutions opened with the regularity that new gas stations or motels open today. Rarely indeed did they close; one did close, however, when a revolution erupted in Nicaragua and the sisters were literally driven out.

Mother went to Central America to figure out the next move. There was always more need than she could supply; she felt as though she confronted a dragon who, when one head was cut off, sprouted a dozen more in its place. She saw to it that all the sisters who had been in Nicaragua went where there was the greatest need for their services, and then with one sister companion, she set off to another place of need, Buenos Aires.

The two religious had to disembark at Valparaiso, Chile, and from there cross the Andes, going over peaks 24,000 feet high, clad in fur-lined cloaks, the gift of a kind friend. First, they traveled by train, second, by mule-drawn coach, and then they had to leave the coach and mount mules. They went some distance, when an order came for everyone to alight. A narrow chasm, thousands of feet deep, lay almost at their feet, threatening to swallow them up. The only way to cross it was to jump it. That would be rather like jumping from skyscraper to skyscraper in modern New York. Men swore, women cried, and Mother prayed. Later, she said she could not have made it, except for a muleteer: "Stretching his feet across the crevice he held me up on one side of the chasm until, with the help of his comrade, he sprang across to the other side. There he drew me . . . to safety."

When at long last Mother and her sister companion reached the journey's end, a priest whom Mother had known in Italy took her to see the archbishop, who needed a school in his diocese. Prospective pupils were everywhere. Obviously, this meant that Mother must make another trip to enlist more sisters, and send them to Buenos Aires.

Tiring as those trips sometimes were, Mother gladly made

them because she always wanted to keep in close contact
with her novitiate. After all, her work depended on the
quality—or the spirituality—of the sisters who were trained
there.

On the way back, she definitely did not recross the Andes,
but left Argentina by ship. In Italy all went smoothly. In
those days, there were always many young girls eager for
the religious life and willing to go far from home to work
in the Lord's vineyard. Some were soon on their way to
Buenos Aires.

While in Europe this time, Mother went to France to start
a house there, hoping that a few graduates of her institutions
might in time enter her Order and serve as French teachers.

When at last she and her recruits were able to return to
the United States, she was met in New York by clamors
for help. She opened another school there and one in
Newark, New Jersey.

Her next trip was to Spain. She wanted to open a school
or an orphanage of her Order there, this time hoping that
some of the graduates of such places might some day join
her Order and so supply Spanish-speaking sisters, who were
now badly needed for her Latin-American institutions.

No less a person than the Spanish queen Maria Christina
welcomed Mother, since the nun's reputation for executive
ability had preceded her. The queen however was soon a
bit miffed because Mother would not allow one of her sisters
to live in the palace to teach Italian to the princesses. Mother
doubted that the luxury of a palace would be the best
environment for sisters seeking spiritual values. In Spain she
soon opened a school and a college in Madrid and an
orphanage in Bilbao.

Writing about Mother Cabrini is like working as a
conductor on a frequently stopping local train, because the
writer is always calling out another place name where

Mother established a new institution. The only difference is that the conductor probably doesn't miss any of the stops, while the writer almost surely does miss some of Mother's.

Was there mention of the school she started in Panama? At any rate, Mother did have a school there, and when revolution broke out in Panama while she was in Spain, the school was closed. Mother hurried to Central America from Europe to pick up the pieces. With the sisters who had staffed the now-defunct school, she opened two new houses—one on the Pampas River, the other on the Paraná River.

More travel followed—to Rio de Janeiro, to São Paulo, to Italy, and to the United States, where she went to the West Coast. There were a number of Italian miners in Oregon, and ecclesiastical authorities felt that she was exactly the right person to serve the needs of the miners and their families.

Since there were fairly frequent mine accidents that injured workers, the first and most pressing need seemed to be a hospital. She established that, and then a school where the Italian-speaking children could learn English and, more important, their religion.

In Oregon a signal event occurred! She became an American citizen! The year was 1909. Hence, in 1946, when she was canonized by Pius XII, she was the first American citizen (though a naturalized one) declared to be a saint by the Catholic Church.

From Oregon she went to Chicago, where she bought a hotel and converted it into a much-needed hospital—her first venture in that city, one that was to be followed by others in due time.

After Chicago came New Orleans and then Scranton, Pennsylvania, where she worked with Italian miners, then back to the West Coast to establish a school in Seattle,

Washington. During this period, traveling from Denver to New Orleans, some desperados shot at the train, and a bullet crashed through the window by which Mother was sitting. Why wasn't she struck? Her explanation was, "It would normally have hit me in the head, but the Sacred Heart intervened." She wasn't even cut by flying glass from the window.

When her shuttle journeys brought her to the East Coast again, she had a different sort of contact with criminals. She arranged for her sisters to visit and try to bring spiritual help to Italian immigrant prisoners in Sing Sing prison.

Where was the "frail" girl? This woman, Frances Xavier Cabrini, seemed a dynamo. One has to agree with her that she thrived on hard work, and one has to acknowledge how right she was in taking as her motto: "I can do all things in him who strengtheneth me" (Phil 4:13). When the twenty-fifth anniversary of her Order arrived, she had fifty houses in eight countries.

Now was it time to retire?

Emphatically not! During the next ten years, she went on without let up. By the time she died, she had founded a total of sixty-seven houses in the space of thirty-five years—one for each of her sixty-seven years of life—and they were served by a total of 1,500 sisters.

In her last years, she had word that a smallpox epidemic ravaged one of her convents in Brazil, so she hurried there to assess the situation and to nurse the ill sisters. Happily, she did not contract the disease herself, but she did develop malaria. On her next trip to Europe, her illness prevented her from traveling to her English convent and to others on her original itinerary. However, when she returned to New York, she was able to plunge into the work of a fund-raising campaign for a new Columbus Hospital. One early contributor, the Italian government, granted her a handsome annual subsidy.

But now, at last, her "frailty" was becoming reality, and she suffered from an intermittent fever. A problem demanding her attention called her to Colorado. The mountain air there seemed to benefit her, and her health improved enough for her to be able to go on to Seattle to establish another orphanage. From Seattle, she went to Chicago.

On this visit to the windy city, she performed none of her usual monumental feats. As Christmas neared that year, 1917, she allowed herself the leisure to write cards to her many far-flung friends. One of the sisters remarked that the biblical verse she was writing on them wasn't particularly appropriate because "It sounds as though you're sending greetings from heaven." The verse was "Send forth thy light and thy truth: they have conducted me, and brought me unto thy holy hill, into thy tabernacles" (Ps 42 Douai). Mother smiled and said, "It will do." Then, a few days before Christmas, she spent long hours helping to wrap candy for the 500 children of her school. Since America had entered the great World War the previous spring, some foods, including sugar, were scarce. Mother had exclaimed, "Christmas won't be Christmas for the children without some sweets", and she managed to get candy. The day that she wrapped it was her last full day on earth.

The next day, December 22, 1917, she died of a hemorrhage.

10

A BRILLIANT STAR

Eve Lavallière

(1866–1929)

Unwanted! No quality of life! An abused child! That describes Eve Lavallière. Her story goes from bawdy drama to bawdy drama, like a soap opera, culminating when she witnessed her father murder her mother and then commit suicide. A few years later, however, her life changed and finally went on to shining success.

This child, later known as Eve Lavallière, began life as Eugénie Marie Fénoglio. She was born in the French Mediterranean seaport of Toulon. Her father, Emile, was a cutter and her mother, Albanie, was a seamstress, and each was a skilled craftsman. The little girl Eugénie did not experience poverty, but she did experience degradation. Emile was an alcoholic, and when he was drunk, which was often, he became violent. Then he would bully and beat his wife and his two children, Eugénie and her older brother, Léon.

The abused trio lived in fear, wondering each night in what state Emile would come home. When he was actually there, Eugénie said, "I sat in my little chair scarcely daring to breathe. I didn't want him to notice me." There were times when Madame Fénoglio could stand it no longer; then she would gather up the two children and dash with them to the railroad station to catch a train for Perpignan where she had relatives.

In a few days Emile would sober up and come to his wife, begging her to return home, promising not to touch another drop for the rest of his life. Albanie would always relent and agree to give him one more chance. No doubt he was sincere and truly meant his promises at the time, but the craving for alcohol sooner or later invariably proved too much for him, and then there would be a replay of the same sad, sickening pattern.

All this of itself was enough to make little Eugénie miserable, still she had to bear more. Her distraught mother had not welcomed her birth and actually seemed to dislike her; no matter what she did, the harried woman constantly found fault with her and showed a marked preference for Léon, while he, taking his cue from his mother, was cruel to his sister with the dreadful unconscious cruelty that only children can show.

Even when Eugénie entered school, there was no relief. The sisters who taught her did not understand this strange, withdrawn little girl with the huge luminous dark eyes and elfin face; they must have subconsciously labeled her "daughter of the drunkard" and expected the worst. Once she lost a comb, and knowing that her erratic mother would whip her if she asked for another, she stole a comb from a schoolmate. Her "crime" was discovered, and not only did she get a beating at home but her reputation as the school's reprobate was confirmed; after that she was suspected of anything at all that went wrong. She was sometimes punished for acts she never committed.

Once when accused falsely of stealing, one of the sisters, never dreaming that the child was innocent, urged Eugénie in a kind way to confess, for "open confession is good for the soul". Not knowing what to do, the child did make the bogus confession. The sister in charge, who likewise never dreamed that Eugénie was innocent, devised an odd and surely a cruel punishment. She made a placard, wrote the word THIEF on it in capital letters, affixed the placard to Eugénie's dress, and made the child walk home through the city streets. When she arrived, she was beaten by both her mother and her father.

The first relief from her misery came when she was ten years old and she was sent to boarding school in Perpignan. There, in a new environment, she blossomed into a happy child, with pixielike charm. She also developed into a rather religious child, and she was ecstatically happy on the day of her first Communion.

The time went by too swiftly, and just a few years later, she had to return to the old sordid mess at home. Since Eugénie didn't know how to escape physically, she tried to escape mentally. She retreated into her own fantasy world. Not only did she read innumerable books and imagine herself as the heroine in them, but she made up original tales and dramas. Then she began gathering the neighborhood children together and putting on shows to dramatize some of her plays. She designed, sewed, and fitted the costumes too, shortly becoming a proficient seamstress. The audience for the plays was made up of proud, loudly applauding parents, so every production seemed to be a huge success.

Things at home, however, were no better, and since alcoholism is a progressive disorder, Emile was drinking more frequently and more heavily than ever. Eugénie's older brother, Léon, joined the French navy to get away, and Albanie announced to her husband that she was breaking with him for good, and she set up a separate household for herself and Eugénie in Perpignan.

Once there, Eugénie, now a young lady, adopted dress-making as a trade. Meanwhile, Emile, in his few sober intervals, came to his wife and begged her to take him back.

At first she refused; indeed, she once called the police to keep him off the premises.

But Emile was persistent. He kept after his wife through the months, promising time after time to give up drink. At length she agreed to let him at least visit her, and she even prepared his favorite dishes for dinner. The date was March 16, 1884.

The dinner went smoothly, and afterward some strolling musicians happened to play beneath the windows, so the scene seemed all the more mellow. Emile told Eugénie to go out onto the balcony and throw coins to the musicians. She stayed a moment to enjoy the fresh air that carried a hint of coming spring; then she was aware that her parents were quarreling—she could hear their strident voices. No doubt her mother was again refusing to return to her husband. Unsavory as these quarrels were, they were nothing new.

Then suddenly there was indeed something new! It sounded like a shot. Eugénie wheeled about and ran inside. Her mother lay on the floor, with blood oozing from a hole in her face.

Eugénie never knew whether she screamed or not. She only remembered standing there frozen with horror. Then her father faced her and pointed a revolver straight at her. For a seeming eternity, the two eyed each other, but finally her father shrugged as if to say, "Oh well, why kill her too?" and he raised the gun and, almost nonchalantly it seemed, shot himself.

The now-orphaned eighteen-year-old Eugénie was taken in grudgingly by a succession of relatives in Perpignan, in Marseilles, and in Nice, none of whom wanted the bother of keeping her long. No one cared about her, and, since she had given up the practice of her religion, she figured God did not care about her either. It seemed sensible to her to commit suicide. One evening in Nice, she went down to the banks of a deep stream and stood there looking at the dark water and trying to nerve herself to get it over with; drowning should not be hard—but, oh, the water looked so black.

Something in her ever-expressive face with its lustrous eyes must have betrayed her thoughts. A man who happened to be passing by this quiet spot and whom she had not as yet seen came over to her and asked gently, "Have you had any dinner?"

When she shook her head to imply No, he said, "I am on my way to a restaurant. Please join me."

After the meal, he arranged for her to have a night's lodging and told her that he would meet her in the morning. In the course of the dinner the man had learned that she was interested in the theater, so he arranged for her to meet the director of a traveling theatrical group.

She never saw her Good Samaritan again, but the director, after having her act out a small scene, hired her without further ado. She began touring the French Mediterranean coast, and her audiences found her fascinating.

Naturally, the stage-door Johnnies appeared, and among them was a marquis. He set Eugénie up in an apartment of her own with a maid, and he gave her gifts of jewelry and furs.

Meanwhile, a relative in Perpignan had her listed by the police among missing persons. The marquis, learning of this, feared that if she were found, he would get in trouble for seducing a minor, so he suggested to Eugénie that she change her name.

She was willing. She had read about the beautiful duchess de la Vallière, mistress of Louis XVI, who later left him to become a Carmelite nun, and she liked the sound of the name. She chose it for her new name, except that she spelled the "la" and the "Vallière" as one word, Lavallière.

The name change perhaps added a bit of glamour; at any rate, Eve Lavallière (alias Eugénie Fénoglio) by now had a following. Clearly, she was talented, and she planned to use her talents to bring her further success. She saved her money, and finally without even saying *"Adieu"* to her marquis, she went to Paris, where opportunities were greater. She did not expect success to drop into her lap. She was willing to work for it, and with the money she had saved, she began to study under the finest theatrical coach in Paris. He gave Eve lessons in diction, singing, and dancing. This enabled her to get a job in a musical comedy theater, where the director soon recognized her potential.

From then on, said a biographer, *"elle atteint rapidement la vedette"*, that is, she soon became a star. She was the preeminent stage personality of Paris and indeed of all France, performing in the plays of Capu, Lavedan, Croisset, and, above all, in those of Flers and Caillavet.

Her rise had been aided by the energetic and talented Fernand Samuel, whom many in the theatrical world called "The Magnificent". He had taken Eve under his personal tutelage and seen her through long hours of training. Besides that, he had persuaded writers to tailor their playwriting to suit Eve's special talents. By 1900 she had attained top billing. The press called Fernand's organization "The Iron Troupe" because of its unbroken series of successes.

While all this was going on, Fernand fell in love with Eve, and she most certainly fell in love with him. Despite having had men friends since she was eighteen, friends who supplied her with every luxury, Fernand was a new experience; she truly cared for him, and she bore him a daughter, whom they named Jeanne.

Eve was probably happier than she had ever before been.

However, the happiness did not last. Fernand, despite genuine fondness for Eve, was not entirely faithful. When Eve discovered this, she broke up the personal relationship with him, though she continued to work with him professionally because of the exigencies of the situation. Fernand took custody of little Jeanne, and Eve seldom saw the child.

The next man to play an important role in her life was the wealthy German baron Georg von Lucius. Although he was married, he begged Eve to marry him as soon as he could divorce his wife. Once in a weak moment she agreed, but soon afterward she said that she did not mean it. When World War I broke out, his government sent him to its embassy in Stockholm, but he still kept in touch with Eve and sent her large sums of money regularly.

Eve did not know what she wanted from life. She had wealth and acclaim. The French drama critics wrote glowingly about her: "Lavallière is an exquisite animal." "The little Fénoglio girl, with her bobbed hair, chic figure, insouciant manner, and spontaneity, electrifies her audience." A reporter from the *Chicago Examiner* declared, "She is the liveliest thing I have seen in many a long day." An English journalist said of her, "She is a symbol of the city (Paris), witty, elegant, enigmatic, audacious." And she was described as "slender, small, light, full of curious, alert, definite grace. . . . Her most noticeable quality, even more so than her beautiful eyes . . . is the exceptional beauty of her speaking voice." Then another critic noted her hands and the way she used them "not so much as a graceful or pretty movement, as a movement which symbolizes well her imaginative power and the willpower to create with her hands what she imagines in her mind."

Yes, she was riding the wave of success, but she was not exhilarated, she was depressed. She went to England briefly to raise money for the Red Cross and perhaps pull herself out of the depression. Her efforts helped the Red Cross, not herself. When she returned to France, her depression was deeper. One night after she attended an elegant dinner at a French chateau, she slipped outside and made her way in the dark to the banks of a stream of water, again considering, though not committing, suicide. Not long after, when a successful performance ended, she walked to the banks of the Seine with the same death wish. This time she leaned over the parapet and prepared to jump when a hand was laid on her shoulder, and an older man, a day laborer, asked, "Madame, may I help?"

Eve answered, "*Merci* . . . no, I don't think so."

The man took a second look and exclaimed, "*Mon Dieu!* You're Eve Lavallière! I am one of your greatest fans. Come, please come, let me walk you home."

She went with him. But the depression had not left her. Indeed, when Fernand died, it was worse. She loved him despite his unfaithfulness to her. But at least she now hoped that her daughter would join her. That was not to be, for Jeanne had become a lesbian and was hostile to her straight mother.

World War I still being in progress, Eve threw herself into the war effort; she performed benefit after benefit for the troops, traveling through France and England until she was physically exhausted. That fact did not stop her from signing a lucrative contract in May 1917, which called for her to go on tour to the United States in the fall. Since she was unusually tired, she decided to spend the intervening time, the summer, in the country resting. She rented a large, handsome chateau and took with her servants and a young Belgian war orphan who served as a sort of companion. The village priest, who was agent for the chateau owners, negotiated the rental contract. He asked her to come to his church for Mass the next Sunday.

Eve found herself agreeing to do so, though it had been years since she had entered a church. A few days later, once in the tiny church, she entered a pew just below the pulpit. The priest, a man with about as much subtlety as a bulldozer, directed his sermon at Eve; talking about fallen-away Catholics and conversions, he never took his eyes from her. She did not know whether to be amused or angry.

Then that afternoon the priest arrived by bicycle at the chateau and had the gall to ask, "How did you like my sermon?"

He must have been disconcerted when she ignored its content, and answered, "Father, you don't know how to preach. You shout!"

Although he protested that she was criticizing form, not substance, he humbly took an elocution lesson from her.

The very next day, he returned, and though he began his conversation with small talk, he very soon blurted out what was on his mind: "What a pity you don't have the Faith!"

Eve answered coolly, "I once had faith in the devil." In fact, she told the priest, she had gone in for spiritualism and with a medium had tried to contact Satan. She had suggested a pact with the fiend: she would bring him recruits if he would keep her young looking and beautiful for another twenty years. "But", she sighed, "the devil has not kept me young looking. There were signs of aging." Eve ended by saying, "Spiritualism is a fraud and there are no devils."

The priest did not marshal any theological arguments, he just kept protesting loudly, "Oh yes, there are devils."

Eve smiled imperturbably and let him protest. But after he had gone, the thought struck her with appalling force: there are indeed devils. I've seen their work in my past. But if there are devils, then there must be a God. And if there is a God, what am I doing with the life he gave me?

The next day, the priest appeared again. He told Eve that

she baffled him. All he could do was pray for her, and he had been doing that steadily since the day she arrived. Then, as direct as usual, he gave her a life of Mary Magdalen and said, "Read this on your knees. Let's see what God can do for a woman like you!"

Actually, Eve did read the book, and she was touched. She began to cry. She wanted faith.

The next time the priest called at the chateau, she astounded him by forthwith beginning to confess her sins and to tell him of her past.

The priest interrupted, "Wait, Mademoiselle! Wait for the confessional. Besides, you're Eve Lavallière. Your life is public. You're a public sinner, and I don't know that I, a simple parish priest, can absolve you. Then, you've delved in spiritualism. That's a reserved sin, and I'd have to get permission from the archbishop to give you absolution."

Of course the priest soon did get the required permission, did absolve Eve, and in June of 1917 she received Communion for the first time in many, many years. All this revolutionized her life. She canceled her American tour and then decided to give up the stage altogether.

The priest advised her against the move, but she said, "I must because I plan to enter the Carmelite Order."

Actually, she was never able to do this. Wherever she applied for admittance, she was turned down on two counts: she was too frail for the austere life (she had been ailing of late) and her past would bring unwanted publicity to the convent.

Disappointed, she returned to Paris and sold her two apartments, the works of art she had accumulated over the years, and her personal jewelry. The money from these sales she gave to the poor.

Meanwhile, the theater-going public did not know what had happened to her. Wild rumors circulated: she had

murdered a lover; a man had been forcing himself on her
so she had temporarily gone into hiding; she was still
grieving over Fernand's death and wanted to be alone for
a while; she was involved in espionage with her former
lover, the Baron von Lucius. The French police took the last
rumor seriously and summoned her for cross-examination.
Since the wealthy Baron had never ceased to send her
money, the suspicion was justified.

Actually, after some months of flitting here and there, she
settled down in a quiet corner of France and joined the Third
Order Secular of St. Francis. But she wanted to give her
life more completely to God. True, her health seemed no
longer robust, but she dreamed of working in the missions.
She went to Tunisia in northern Africa, and for seven
months of each year from 1921 to 1924, she served as
member of a nursing team, tending sick Arab children.

Then her health broke, and she returned to France to lead
a quiet life much like that of a contemplative nun. In 1927
she became seriously ill. She suffered from what the doctors
called African fever and then from peritonitis. During the
next year and a half until her death on July 10, 1929, Eve
endured excruciating pain. She suffered not only patiently
but gratefully. Minute after minute, hour after hour, she
thanked God for the opportunity to atone for some of her
sins. On the day she died, the attending priest said to her,
"God has pardoned you because you loved much. Depart
in peace, O liberated Christian soul."

11

GENIUS AT WORK

Marie Sklodowska Curie
(1867-1934)

"The actual record of Marie Curie's life is epic"—so the *Chicago Tribune* once wrote. Giant among giants, she was the first person, man or woman, to receive two Nobel Prizes. More awesome yet, she began and, with the collaboration of her husband, completed work that led to what some scientists called "the most important discovery of modern science".

Despite the world acclaim that she received, she remained a semirecluse who found fulfillment in her work, not in the recognition of it. As for the wealth that might have accrued to her, that meant nothing to her one way or the other. Einstein declared, "Marie Curie is, of all celebrated beings, the only one whom fame has not corrupted."

She was born Marie Sklodowska in Poland, which at that time, even as today, was dominated by Russia. Her family, although of the petty nobility, was far from wealthy. Her father's slim salary as a professor of physics was the sole support of his wife and four children. They lived with severe simplicity but with great contentment. Nominally they were Roman Catholics. Religion, however, played but a minor role in their lives, and when her mother died, the heartbroken Marie put God aside, not because she was bitter but because she was baffled by his unknowable designs.

The Sklodowska's focused on the learning that could be

laboratory tested. It was their life's passion, their labor, their recreation, and their quasi-religion.

Marie's older sister Bronya, though she yearned to go to the Sorbonne in Paris to study medicine, lacked the money. Marie dreamed of the Sorbonne too, so she proposed that she, on graduation from school, take a job and, with her savings, add to the small sum that their father would be able to give Bronya so that she could finance her dream. Then when Bronya had become a doctor, she in turn could help Marie.

The plan worked. Eventually, Marie reached Paris and the Sorbonne. Professors lecturing in French meant hard going for the young Polish girl, but she relished every moment of her classes, and she went back to Bronya's home in the evenings, eager to resume study. Broyna was now married, and Marie's one regret was that the family life about her tended to distract her from her books, so after a few months, she moved out with reluctance and rented a cheap garret room. There she lived on a tight schedule: school by day, public library by evening until its close at 10 P.M., home and study until 2 A.M.

Often she forgot to eat, and when she did remember, her slim purse inhibited her. She subsisted mainly on bread and tea. The result was anemia and fainting spells. So Bronya brought Marie back to her home. The girl now ate well, but nothing changed her study habits, and she systematically attained her goals: a master's in physics, a master's in chemistry, and a master's in mathematics, plus a rare command of the French language.

So it was time to return to her loving father in Poland and find a job there. But shortly after her homecoming, the unexpected happened. A family friend submitted Marie's name for a cash scholarship, and Marie bested the other contestants. This lagniappe meant she could go back to the Sorbonne to work for a doctorate.

At this stage she gave no thought to love or marriage. Probably, if she had so much as glanced their way, some of the young men in her classes might have been interested in the slender girl with the serious, deep-set gray eyes, the ash-blonde hair, and the determined chin, but she was hardly aware of their existence. Indeed, she showed little interest at first in the tall French scientist Pierre Curie, who was decidedly interested in her. He found someone to introduce her to him, and he began to call. Characteristically, his first gift to her—and one she truly appreciated—was a scientific treatise. After that, she did notice him, and one evening he said to her, "I wish you would come with me to visit my parents."

He described his family life and his childhood to her, and it seemed amazingly like her own. Yes, everything seemed to be drawing them together, but when Pierre proposed, Marie felt she must refuse. She explained that although they shared scientific and humanitarian dreams and goals, there was something they could not share. She was Polish, and the Poles were under the Russian heel, so she had a fierce patriotism that could not be his. Her dream and her duty were to prepare herself for work and then return to her country to serve it in some capacity.

Still, Pierre quietly and persistently argued his case, offering to move to Poland. Marie refused that offer, but by year's end she found that she could not withstand his love—nor her own. They married in 1895.

They were a matched pair—friends, lovers, coworkers.

Pierre, professor and director of laboratories at the Municipal School of Physics and Chemistry, made a modest, barely adequate salary, but living economically didn't bother them. Indeed, it did not bother them when, after their

baby Irene was born, they had to make stringent retrench-
ments to hire a nursemaid for the child while Marie worked
on her doctorate. This was necessary, although Dr. Curie,
Sr., Pierre's widower father, lived with them and was a most
loving and vigilant grandfather.

Marie's studies introduced her to the scientific publications
of Henri Becquerel. He had discovered that uranium, an
element found in pitchblende, spontaneously, without
exposure to light, emitted rays of an unknown nature. He
could not explain the phenomenon, so she experimented
with it, hoping to learn more and to write her dissertation
on it.

The laboratory where she worked—really an old shed—
was bitter cold and ill equipped, but she spent day after
shivering day there, working with almost superhuman
perseverance as she measured the power of ionization of the
rays. Finally, her amassed data indicated that the rays were
a hitherto unknown element and that they had an atomic
property.

But did other substances besides uranium have these rays?

She set for herself a Herculean task: she would experiment
with all known chemical elements to find out. As her
daughter wrote years later, she was endowed with "a
terrible patience".

To her amazement, she discovered that the other elements
too emitted rays. This monumental discovery was only the
beginning of her gigantic task. She had to verify each
experiment by rerunning it several times. After all, she
might have made error in former experiments. Then she had
to determine the nature of these rays.

After multitudinous experiments, she came to an audacious
conclusion, which she announced to the scientific world: the
radiation came from a probable new chemical element
endowed with what she called radioactivity. She named the

new element polonium to honor her native land. It was step 1 toward radium discovery!

Now doggedly continuing experiments, she tackled the task of isolating this new element, and Pierre, in view of the importance of her project and the immensity of the work it entailed, abandoned his own experimentation with crystals and collaborated with Marie. The collaboration was so close that there was no separation of his work from hers, her work from his.

Pitchblende residue needed for their experiments was costly, and although Marie as well as Pierre now had a teaching job, their combined salaries could not cover expenses. This posed a dilemma until the Austrian government presented them with the material and somehow they scraped together money to pay for its transportation to France.

Exactly forty-five months after Marie had announced the existence of a probable new element, having treated no less than eight tons of pitchblende residue, she succeeded in preparing a decigram of pure radium. The formerly incredulous colleagues had to concede that radium existed. Voilà! There it was!

Recognizing genius, the University of Geneva offered Pierre a teaching position at twice his present salary. The Curies were ready to jump at the offer until they realized the sad truth: they would have to interrupt their research. As conscientious scientists, they felt they could not do that.

They continued to drudge away. Their only distraction was an interval each evening with their child, Irene, and a short summer vacation in the country. They were both nature lovers.

About this time, Marie's father died. She went to Poland for the funeral with a sad heart, made the sadder because she had not found a way to see more of him during his lifetime. Through letters and reports, he had followed her work closely and understood, as few did, its great signifi- cance. Shortly before he died, he wrote her, "Now you are in possession of salts of pure radium. If you consider the amount of work that has been spent to obtain it, it is certainly the most costly of chemical elements."

Back in Paris after the funeral, she resumed her grueling work. Lacking traditional religion, the Curies had in effect substituted science for it, or at least they substituted for it the benefits that science could bring mankind. Their substitute for religion was extremely demanding. Often it begrudged them time to eat properly or to get sufficient sleep, so their health suffered. Pierre had bouts of pain, and Marie, when she became pregnant, experienced, to her keen disappointment, a miscarriage.

Although she suspected her long working hours were at least partially responsible for the disaster, she could not see how she could manage with fewer hours. Besides teaching and laboratory work, she as well as Pierre had to write reports if their discoveries were to help others. From 1899 to 1904, the Curies published thirty-two scientific papers. A biographer says that they freely gave "explanations and technical advice to their colleagues. In several countries, research workers rushed into the search for unknown radioactive elements . . . a pursuit to which we owe mesothorium, radiothorium, ionium, protactinium, and radio-lead."

England, Germany, Austria, Denmark, and other countries wrote for information, especially after the Curies discov- ered that radium cured growths, tumors, and some types of cancer.

In 1902 the Academy of Science awarded the Curies a large sum for "the extraction of radioactive matter". They began to purify five tons of ore. A French industrialist, envisioning his factory producing radium to sell to doctors, offered the Curies a clean, bright laboratory. He was not the only one with such an idea. People the world over, including some in the United States, clamored for a connection with the Curies' techniques.

Now, Marie and Pierre could give the information gratis, or they could patent their process and make millions. But to them the latter course was out of the question; it was "contrary to the scientific spirit". They chose, then, continued poverty and hardship over certain wealth and comfort.

But they had no choice about fame. France, Switzerland, England, and the United States all rushed to give them awards. Then in 1903 they received the coveted Nobel Prize together with Henri Becquerel. Newspapers everywhere touted their triumph.

Later, Pierre spoke in Stockholm for Marie and himself. He explained the consequences of the radium discovery. In physics, it modified the fundamental principles of mechanics. In chemistry, it suggested hypotheses on the source of energy. In geology and in meteorology, it explained certain formerly unexplained phenomena. In biology, it promised an effective treatment for certain types of cancer. Again, newspapers headlined the story, and honors and fame snowballed. England awarded the couple the Davey Medal, and the University of Paris created a chair in physics for Pierre.

Finally, fame and prize money changed poverty to comfort.

The dark side of the fame was loss of privacy and of peace. Telephone calls, letters, and visits cut into their work hours.

About this time, Marie became pregnant again, and for once in her adult life, she slowed down. The baby, a healthy girl whom they named Eve, arrived without mishap.

A pleasant interval followed. The couple began to take time for social life, because Parisian confreres and scientists from other countries called to discuss scientific matters with them. During the Easter holidays, they went off for delightful days in the country. They rode their bicycles and plucked wild flowers and thoroughly enjoyed themselves.

Then back in the city again—and tragedy. On a rainy April day in 1906, Pierre attended a luncheon of the Association of Professors in the Faculty of Science. Afterward, crossing the street in his usual abstracted, absent-minded way, he stepped into the path of a heavy wagon drawn by two horses. It knocked him to the hard cobblestones, and one iron wheel of the wagon ran over his head, crushing his skull as though it were an eggshell. In a fleeting moment, the great scientist lay dead.

A representative of the Republic of France as well as the dean of the faculty went to the Curie home to notify Marie. She received the news as though she had not heard it or had not understood it. She uttered no sound.

She never could voice her deep grief, but a day or so later, she put down on paper what she could not say aloud. She wrote, "It is the end of everything, everything, everything."

After that, almost to Marie's surprise, life went on. She must have remembered that Pierre had once said, "If one of us dies, even if the other has to go on like a body without a soul, the other one must work just the same." She continued their joint work. Pierre had always dreamed of a modern laboratory, and she hoped that before she died, she could see one built.

But how was she to fare financially—this thirty-eight-year-old widow with two children and her father-in-law who lived with them?

In recognition of the joint Curie work, the government of France offered her a pension, but she refused it, saying,

"I'm young enough to earn my living and that of my children."

The Sorbonne, which had never had a woman on its faculty, offered Marie the chair created for her late husband. She, rather than any other scientist, was capable of filling it. She wrote in her diary, "I am offered the position of successor to you, my Pierre. . . . I have accepted. . . . I am better off there than anywhere else. I can conceive of nothing any more that could give me personal joy except perhaps scientific work—and even there, no, because I could not endure you not to know of it."

Though devastated by grief, Marie still struggled to give her children the pleasant life she wanted for them. Marie's daughter Eve declared in her biography of her mother that Marie managed to give them a passionate interest in science and a willingness to work. She also took great interest in their schooling; she not only followed it, she took an active part in the teaching as well. She also insisted on their taking physical exercise.

In 1910 she published the 971-page-long "Treatise on Radioactivity". She also collected, edited, and wrote a biographical preface for a book that she entitled simply "Works of Pierre Curie". She undertook to isolate radium metal—a departure from her former work of preparing salts of radium.

Soon too she published "Classification of the Radioelements" and a "Table of Radioactive Constants" and then prepared the first international standard of radium.

France, anxious to give her the highest honor possible, offered her the Cross of the Legion of Honor. Modest Marie refused it. She did accept, however, many other honors and prizes. The appendix of one biography lists honorary degrees bestowed on Marie by nearly every nation—104 of them, no less! In 1911 she received the Nobel Prize in chemistry. It was the first time in history that anyone had received the Nobel Prize twice.

To her great joy, also, her dream and Pierre's of the laboratory, the Institute of Radium, was built by the nation on the Rue Pierre Curie. It comprised two parts, one the laboratory of radioactivity, and the other the Curie therapy center for cancer treatment studies. She directed it.

Then came World War I and sudden turmoil! Paris itself was threatened by the onrushing German army. A short time before, Marie had sent her two children to Brittany, and she decided now to leave them in that comparatively quiet spot.

She had in the past lectured on Roentgen's discovery of x-rays, but its use was not yet widespread. Convinced of its diagnostic value, Marie, with funds from the Union of the Women of France, fitted out a radiological car with x-ray apparatus and a dynamo, making it like a mobile minihospital, and she herself, along with a military driver, went to the front with it. It was the only such vehicle to care for the host of wounded evacuated toward Paris during the battle of the Marne. She begged more such cars from wealthy people and fitted each—twenty in all—with x-ray apparatus, and these cars, now called "little Curies", went to Verdun, Amiens, Ypres, and so on.

Often she herself drove to the field hospital, and it was she who regulated the apparatus, focused on the torn flesh, and took the x-ray pictures that showed the surgeon the shell fragment to be extracted. She would be shut up in the darkroom for hours, as a seemingly endless succession of men was carried in one after the other. Of course, she often had to skip meals or sleep in a tent and often too she had to crank a car or change a tire.

Still, Marie wanted to do more. She put the money she had received for her second Nobel Prize into the war effort.

She used the emanations of her radium to cure the kinds of scars and lesions susceptible to its help. Then because more x-ray technicians were needed in the military hospitals, she inaugurated a course in radiology. Among her students were twenty soldiers of the American Expeditionary Forces.

Finally, the war ended! No one was more exultant than Marie about the Allied victory. She was overjoyed too because her native Poland was free at last from Russia. She wrote to her brother about "the resurrection of our country which has been our dream". Mercifully, she could not envision the future and worse Russian enslavement under Communism.

The war had disorganized her scientific work and had somewhat impoverished her. Her salary as professor and as director of the Institute, although it covered living expenses plus the education of her daughters, didn't allow many luxuries. Not that this worried her; hard at work on a book that she had been asked to write on "Radiology in War", she didn't think of luxuries. Then in the summer after the war, she relaxed—insofar as she could relax—and she and her girls took a place in a quiet little village on the Brittany coast where they could swim.

Back in Paris by fall, an American woman reporter interviewed her. When the woman learned that the famed scientist no longer owned a gram of radium, she was appalled, but Marie explained that she had given away her radium and could not afford to replace it.

Returning to the United States, the reporter organized a National Marie Curie Campaign to raise money to buy Marie radium. The U.S. president was to present it personally. This meant that retiring Marie had to travel abroad and endure not only being lionized at a White House reception but acclaimed by cheering crowds, taken from place to place to be "exhibited", and written up with screaming headlines, "Benefactress of the Human Race" and "World's Great Scientist". Then too, it seemed she must constantly make gracious and public thank-you speeches.

While she shrank from the exhausting hoopla, she soon realized that by publicity she could raise money for her cherished scientific projects. Therefore, after the U.S. trip she allotted some time to giving public lectures and to making an occasional hasty trip to attend some scientific congresses in other places—England, Holland, Italy, Brazil, and Spain. She particularly wanted money for a Polish center for scientific research and for cancer treatment.

Meanwhile, the French, impressed by the honor paid everywhere to the woman it considered its own Mme. Curie, began to appreciate her the more. Again the nation offered Marie its exalted award, the Cross of the Legion of Honor. Again she refused it, partly, one suspects, because Pierre had never received it and she didn't want to surpass him.

In time there was money to build the center in Poland, and Marie was asked to lay the cornerstone. She did so gladly. But the center would have no radium unless . . . here Marie thought again of generous America. At her request, the American people came through a second time, and Mme. Curie received a gram of the precious stuff for Poland from the hands of President Hoover.

When she returned to France, what a great surprise! Baron de Rothschild created the Curie Foundation to collect gifts to support the work of the Radium Institute. The doctors of France honored her radium discovery for treatment of cancer by the unprecedented move of electing her to the Academy of Medicine. Then in 1923, the twenty-fifth anniversary of radium's discovery, the French Parliament unanimously passed a law granting her a generous annual pension and her daughters the right of inheritance.

Incidentally, that anniversary was celebrated with speeches and ceremonies, which the president of the Republic of France and other notables attended. Marie wore a rather shabby black dress, indistinguishable from other such black dresses she had worn through the years. With her pension she could have been fashionably attired, but she never thought of dress. She was busy building a factory for experimentation with ores.

Although she was growing older, she didn't curtail teaching, writing, or experiments. Between 1919 and the year of her death, 1934, she published thirty-four scientific papers. She still spent long hours absorbed in work, so that students, noticing that she had forgotten lunch, would often place a meal in front of her. One of the last works of her lifetime was preparing actinium for the spectrum of alpha rays. The day she worked on that, she didn't stop for dinner but worked on until 2 A.M.

She became ill, and at first thought she had a touch of flu or the grippe. It was far more serious than that, and she was sent to a sanatorium where she died July 4, 1934, at age sixty-seven. The doctor reported the cause to be "aplastic pernicious anemia. The bone marrow did not react, probably because it had been injured by a long accumulation of radiation."

After her death, the book she had been writing was published. Its title was *Radioactivity*.

12

LADY LINDY, AVIATION PIONEER

Amelia Earhart

(1897–1937)

She was in love with the sky! It symbolized the freedom and the scope that she considered the breath of life.

This Kansas-born girl with the boyish wind-swept hair, who was nicknamed Lady Lindy because she looked amazingly like Charles Lindbergh, had a yearning for adventure and a need to reach out to the unknown. Her father encouraged her in this, although he and her mother saw that Amelia received the sort of education suitable for a proper young lady of the period. Amelia attended Ogontz Junior College in Rydal, Pennsylvania, and then Columbia University, and her adventures during her school years were mostly through books.

Then in 1920 when she was twenty-two, her father took her to an air show in Long Beach, California. On that day, Amelia flew! It was the era when flying was still a novelty to the general public, so pilots, in order to earn a few dollars, would take up passengers for a short flight. At Long Beach Amelia—as a passenger, of course—had her first flight. Later, she wrote in her book *For the Fun of It,* "As soon as we left the ground, I knew that I myself had to fly."

She began to take flying lessons, and in 1921 she soloed for the first time. The following year she bought her own plane. Utterly serious about flying, she practiced stalls, spins, forced landings, and flying through fog without instru-

ments. She set a new altitude record for women. Although
for a brief time she did return to Columbia to resume her
premed courses, she soon abandoned them; she knew that
flying was to be her life's work. Still, she was interested
in, and found many things, a challenge, so she had other jobs
on the side.

When she was teaching English in the Denison Settlement
House in Boston in 1928, she had a phone call from another
pilot. He asked, "Would you be interested in doing
something for aviation that might be hazardous?"

Of course she was interested! What was the "hazardous"
something?

The answer came, "Fly the Atlantic."

Lindbergh had done it the year before, 1927, but so far,
no woman had. Unlike Lindbergh, she would fly only as a
passenger. This she found disappointing; she would have
liked to have been the pilot, but Wilmer Stultz was slated
for that job. Amelia's job was to take over for Stultz if the
situation should ever demand it. There was to be a mechanic
aboard, Louis Gordon. The plane was a Fokker C-2,
christened *Friendship.* The project had wealthy backers,
among them Paramount Pictures and the publishing house
of George Putnam.

But before plans could be finalized, she must agree to
certain conditions: once she returned from Europe, she must
make a personal appearance tour across the country and
write a book plus newspaper articles about her experience.

Amelia accepted the conditions, and plans went forward.
The only snag was that bad weather delayed take-off, and
when the plane did depart Boston and then refueled in
Newfoundland, it met a further delay of two weeks. But
at last came the big day when the crew headed for Europe.
It was June 17, 1928.

In the almost twenty-one hours of flight, it was never

necessary for Amelia to take over the controls. Her praise of Stultz' ability was lavish. She cabled President Coolidge, "Success was entirely due great skill of Mr. Stultz (Stop) He was only one mile off course at Valentia after flying blind for two thousand, two hundred forty six miles at average speed of one hundred thirteen MPH."

The plane landed in Wales, and after a day for rest and refueling, the crew flew on to Southampton, England, where they were feted for days on end. Kings and dignitaries heaped praise on the now thirty-year-old American woman, the pioneer who had braved the crossing of wide seas in a tiny plane, but she discounted their words. She had been a mere passenger. Now she wanted to pilot long flights herself.

But topping her agenda was the book she had promised to write about the trans-Atlantic flight. She entitled the book, her first of course, *20 hrs. 40 Min.* (That was the exact length of the flight.) The writing was competent if not brilliant, and the editors of *Cosmopolitan* asked her to write eight articles per year on aviation for their magazine. Then, colleges, universities, and women's clubs deluged her with invitations to lecture.

Although all these activities brought Amelia both affluence and adulation, she still took time from them for flying regularly and she entered aeronautical competitions, often winning prizes. In 1929 she broke the women's speed record. In 1931 she set an autogiro altitude record.

While she was busy with her many activities, George Putnam had asked her to marry him. She said, No. In fact, she said No to his first five proposals, but according to his reckoning, it was his sixth that won the Yes. After that, they were soon married. She was not being arbitrary in holding out so long; it was just that she prized freedom, she wanted adventure, and she feared marriage might rather literally clip her wings.

From the accounts, it does not seem to have been a romantic marriage. Amelia's first love, the sky, remained first. Before the wedding took place, she wrote George a letter saying, "I must exact a cruel promise . . . that you will let me go in a year if we find no happiness together." She added, "I will try my best."

Try her best, she did, and the marriage might be called "happy" in that they lived together amicably between her flights to distant places. She found rather distasteful his desire to capitalize on and commercialize her exploits and her fame.

She made her solo trans-Atlantic flight in 1932. During the four years since her flight with Stultz, she had worked toward this end. One of her biographers said that her study and practice of the "art and technology of aviation during this period was relentless". In those days, navigational equipment was, by today's standards, primitive, and the accumulated data on technical problems were sparse. Pilots learned by trial and error, so Amelia spent hundreds of hours in the air, trying to discover the best techniques by way of experimentation.

Still, on her solo trans-Atlantic flight, she encountered some difficulties (not unusual in those pioneer days); her altimeter malfunctioned, she ran into bad icing conditions, and at one point she had a blazing manifold, but all were brought under control and she made excellent time, landing in Ireland just fourteen hours and fifty-six minutes after take-off in Newfoundland. She had bettered Lindbergh's flying time considerably.

As at the end of her previous Atlantic flight, she was feted by the high and the mighty, and as then, she had only the clothes on her back. To avoid adding weight to the plane, she had even skimped on the food she carried aboard, for she said, "A pilot whose plane falls into the Atlantic is not consoled by caviar sandwiches."

When she returned to the United States, she was entertained at the White House by President and Mrs. Hoover, and she was presented with the Distinguished Flying Cross before a joint session of the Senate and the House.

Some months later, in the summer of 1932, she was off again. This time she established a speed record for women for a nonstop flight from coast to coast across the United States. The next year she broke her own record by two hours. Then in 1935 she made the first solo flight over the long stretch from Honolulu to California. That same year she was the first to fly from Mexico City to New York.

It was in 1937 that she began the flight that she hoped was to encircle the world. A fascinated public followed her reported progress as, with her navigator, Fred Noonan, accompanying her, she flew from California to Brazil, to Africa, to India, and to New Guinea. Then she began the longest over-water leg of 25,000 miles from New Guinea, headed for Howland Island. She radioed reports of her progress. Then suddenly, silence!

The world held its breath. Time lengthened, and still no more word came. What had happened? Was she lost at sea? Where was she? And if she had been forced down, where was the wreckage of her plane?

The government swung into action. The search for her was the longest and most expensive in history. President Roosevelt sent the carrier *Lexington* and the battleship *Colorado* and a dozen other vessels in search of her. Some 262,281 square miles of the Pacific were searched by ships and planes. They found not the slightest trace of Amelia or of her plane!

The intrepid Lady Lindy, who had apparently vanished like

smoke, became a larger-than-life legend. Hollywood made a movie about her, *Flight for Freedom.*

Twenty-four years later, a woman was quoted in a California newspaper as saying that back in 1937, shortly after the famed disappearance, she had seen two American aviators fitting the description of Amelia and her navigator on the Pacific island of Saipan in the Marianas.

The statement aroused the curiosity of a media personality, Fred Goerner, and he soon convinced others that the story was worth investigating. CBS, the *San Mateo Times,* the Scripps-Howard League of Newspapers, and the Associated Press spent enormous sums of money backing Goerner in an investigation that lasted six years and involved almost unbelievably painstaking work.

Goerner wrote a fascinating book about it. He interviewed countless natives on the island, and many testified that the Japanese had brought a man and a woman of Earhart's and Noonan's description to Saipan after their plane was forced down. Back in 1937 the Japanese were already preparing for the war that began at Pearl Harbor, and (so some testimony went) they suspected that these two were spies for the United States government. The man was executed, and the woman was thrown into a miserable prison where not long afterward she died of disease.

Startling as these revelations were, more startling is Goerner's statment that it is almost certain that Amelia was indeed a spy for the United States. If Japan were preparing for war with us and if Japan were building airstrips and airbases on certain Pacific islands, the United States needed to know about them, and Amelia, though she had begun to plan for her around-the-world flight as a means of furthering aviation and as a personal adventure, would patriotically have acceded to her government's request to note what she could of Japanese war preparations. The government assigned some of its top experts ostensibly to "advise" Amelia about her itinerary. It was they who wanted her to go to Howland Island, toward which she was headed when she disappeared; she had not originally intended to go there.

After the disappearance, the government, in an unprecedented move, spent vast sums of money trying to trace her, a private citizen—and it spent the money in the middle of the worst depression in history. Most conclusive of all, after six years of trying, Goerner could not break through a wall that the government seemed to erect to thwart his investigations. The files on Amelia Earhart are stamped "Top Secret", and Goerner found out that their contents cannot be seen by an ordinary citizen.

Amelia Earhart Putnam's life remains a mystery story. If she was a spy, she gave her life for her country.

13

OTHER FABULOUS FEMALES

This is the kind of book that could go on and on, because more and more women of the past could always be included. Writing it is like walking toward the rim of the horizon in order to touch the sky. Since that's impossible, the book must stop arbitrarily, but before it does, a few more women must have at least a brief word.

It would be a shame to leave out, for instance, the courageous seventeenth-century Marie Guyard Martin (better known by her name in religion, Mère Marie de L'Incarnation). Having been widowed, having reared her son to young manhood, and having successfully run a business, Marie dreamed of bringing the gospel to the natives of the newly discovered lands across the sea.

Her confessor dismissed that idea as a castle-in-the-air fantasy and in effect advised, "'Get you to a nunnery' and stay there." She joined the Ursulines, and later, by most improbable circumstances, her dream actually did become reality. She procured the necessary ecclesiastical permission, and a friend provided the financial means. In 1639, with a few nuns of kindred spirit, Marie embarked on the three-month voyage that took her to Quebec, where she managed to establish a convent, learn the Indian language, teach the Indians, and compile a French-Huron dictionary and a catechism in the Huron language.

Her *Letters,* collected by her son (a Benedictine monk, who had remained in France) were published serially in Paris and gave an invaluable and vivid picture of Quebec from 1639 to 1671. She lived not only under primitive conditions and with great hardship but never far from the threateningly poised bloody tomahawk of the Hurons. Advice and even pleas to return to France did not sway her; hers was a lifelong commitment.

The brilliant French prelate Bossuet called her "the Teresa of the New World". She is the subject of a book, *Mère Marie of the Ursulines* by Willa Cather (herself a long liberated lady of great stature, one of America's outstanding novelists, a veritable artist with words, and winner of many honors and prizes, among them the *Prix Femina Americain*).

While Mère Marie was toiling in Canada, another French widow, one who never left her native soil, Louise de Marillac de Gras, was transforming the character of Christian charity and greatly expanding it by establishing permanent institutions to put social care on a stable footing. She founded the Sisters of Charity, whose hospitals, orphanages, nursing homes, and other institutions dot our globe like confetti sprinkled with a liberal hand.

Then there was Madeleine Hachard, a pioneer Ursuline like Mère Marie who also merits mention at least in passing. She went to then-French-held New Orleans from France in the 1700s. On the voyage over, pirates attacked the ship, and the captain ordered the nuns aboard to dress as men. When Madeleine arrived in 1727—safely, be it added—she served the convent and the New Orleans settlers as pharmacist, becoming the first person of that profession in what is now the United States. Then she, along with the other sisters in her convent, not only educated the French children in New Orleans but tended orphans whose parents had been killed in an Indian massacre, and they provided shelter for the "casket girls" arriving from France until these young ladies found suitable husbands.

About fifty years later there was the girl patriot Deborah

Sampson, who disguised herself as a man in order to fight in the American War of Independence. (Obviously, the recruits were given no physical examinations in those days.) It was when she was wounded with a musketball through the shoulder and was hospitalized that a doctor discovered her secret. As soon as she was able to travel again, he sent her with a sealed letter to no less a person than George Washington. She knew that the letter would reveal all, so she was fearful that Washington might order court-martial. She was immensely relieved and grateful that he dismissed her with exquisite courtesy. Nonetheless, to her regret, he signed an honorable discharge. After the war, she married, had three children, and became one of America's first lecturers, telling from the platform about her combat duty.

Another patriot of our War of Independence, Ethan Allen, had a liberated lady, Frances Allen, for a daughter. She had the courage to stand up to her father, who was vociferously antireligious. (It was he who wrote the deistic book *Reason: the Only Oracle of Man*, and he whom a minister dubbed "The Great Infidel".) The liberated Frances ignored the fierce opposition of all her nonbelieving family members, even to the extent of going to Canada to join a religious nursing Order, thus becoming the first U.S.-born nun. For that she has her footnote in history; she is mentioned in books and encyclopedias, and a hospital is named in her honor (in Winoosky Park, Vermont).

In the next century, there was the frontierwoman Nellie Cashman Day, the Irish girl who went to California and then on to British Columbia, seeking gold. She found no gold, but she devotedly nursed men ill with scurvy. She is credited with ending the plague by having fresh potatoes shipped in.

Going on to Tombstone, Arizona, she opened first a restaurant, then a hotel while she grubstaked miners for a share of their finds. A good businesswoman, she met with considerable success, yet she still found time for much else. She took in her five orphaned nephews and nieces and reared them. Then she also nursed any who fell ill, and she helped all sorts of people who were "down on their luck". She was nicknamed "the Angel of Tombstone".

She certainly proved the nickname on a prospecting trip in Baja California. She and her companion lost their way and ran out of water. The area was desertlike, so the dozen or so men, seeing only death staring them in the face, were despairing. Not Nellie! She slipped off and walked for miles until, fortuitously, she came on a mission outpost where she was given water, which she carried back to save the lives of the stranded men.

She saved not only men's lives but their souls. Once visiting the Tombstone jail, she talked with five men held for murder, and before they were executed, she persuaded three of them to repent and to become Catholics.

Better known is another frontierwoman, "Calamity Jane" (Martha Jane Canary), who was a rider for the Pony Express and a scout for Custer's forces. She became a heroine for a series of dime novels in the 1880s. (Incidentally, according to one source, she acquired her nickname because she forcefully asserted that anyone who tried to molest her was asking for calamity.)

On the other side of the continent, far from these western women, in Philadelphia to be exact, lived a very different sort of long liberated lady, Katharine Drexel.

Having inherited millions from her banker father, Francis A. Drexel, Katharine felt a responsibility for the ultimate disposal of such a large estate. She wanted to use it to help in proselytizing Indians and Negroes. During a visit to Rome, she had an audience with Pope Leo XIII, and she asked him to recommend a religious Order or an organization to which she might leave a large portion of her fortune for this purpose. The Pope answered her with a question, "Why not become a missionary to these people yourself?"

It was an idea worth pondering over and praying about. In 1891 she started her own Order, using for a convent the Drexel summer home in Torresdale, Pennsylvania. She spent more than $12 million (a sum worth considerably more than today) on the expenses that she and her sisters of the Blessed Sacrament Order incurred as they went out to convert Negroes and Indians and to care for them physically.

On January 26, 1987, Pope John Paul II declared Katharine Drexel "Venerable", a step toward possible canonization.

Rose Hawthorne Lathrop in a different way was also a liberated lady of note. This daughter of famed novelist Nathaniel Hawthorne, being forced to separate from her alcoholic husband, spent the rest of her days in a tremendous work of mercy. Toward the end of the nineteenth century, she became aware of the plight of the cancerous poor in New York, who had no one to care for them. They were not kept in the city hospitals but were sent to Blackwell's Island to find their own place to die. With very little money, Rose moved into a tenement house in New York City and began to take in as many of these unfortunates as she could handle. Soon, other large-hearted women joined her in the work. Finally, the little group (Rose's husband had died by this time) adopted the Rule of the Dominican Order of nuns, calling themselves Servants for the Relief of Incurable Cancer.

Katherine Burton wrote a biography of Rose, entitled *Sorrow Built a Bridge,* and Rose herself wrote *Memories of Hawthorne* and a little book of poems entitled *Along the Shore.*

A contemporary of Rose's was the pedagogic innovator Marie Montessori. After receiving the degree of doctor of medicine from the University of Rome in 1894, she became principal of a school for feebleminded children. She was so successful with these children that she adapted some of her methods for teaching normal children. In 1917 she became director of the Montessori Research Institute in Barcelona, and in 1922 she was made government inspector of schools for Italy. She was the author of several books on education, and her methods are still used in many schools throughout the world.

Another extraordinary teacher and long liberated lady who cannot be left out is Anne Sullivan. Both she and her extraordinary pupil, Helen Keller, deserve much more space than is possible to give them. The lives of Anne and Helen are inextricably intertwined.

Mark Twain said that the two most interesting characters of the nineteenth century are Napoleon and Helen Keller. Helen, who was born a healthy normal baby in Alabama in 1880, fell ill at the age of only nineteen months and as a result lost both hearing and sight. These serious handicaps debarred her from school, so her loving parents hired the young New Englander Anne Sullivan, who had been trained to teach the blind, to instruct their daughter.

No one before Anne had ever attempted to teach so severely handicapped a person as Helen, so many of Anne's methods had to be of her own devising. She taught Helen about birds by taming pigeons and letting the child handle them, about plant life by having Helen drop seeds into a furrow and then bringing her back day after day to feel the growing sprouts.

Being totally deaf and blind, Helen had to identify objects solely by touch or smell. Yet Anne found a way to teach her a concept that the child had not dreamed of: that objects had names. When Helen touched something, Anne quickly "spelled" out the name in the child's palm. Verbs, adverbs, and adjectives were harder to explain, but Anne found ways to do that too. Abstract ideas were another hurdle. In her autobiography, Helen tells about her struggles with the word *love*. She brought violets to Anne, wondering if love was the perfume of flowers. It was a long time before she could grasp the meaning of the word.

Anne taught Helen to trace letters with her fingers and eventually to write. She taught Helen geography by making little mounds in sand for mountains and digging channels and hollows that she filled with water for rivers and lakes. She taught Helen geometry with wire triangles and squares. She taught Helen French, using a French grammar with raised letters. She taught Helen braille, and by using braille books or books with raised letters, Helen was able to read— and she became an avid reader. But one of the most valuable skills that Anne taught Helen was typing. By typing, Helen (always accompanied by Anne, who spelled out the teacher's oral explanations) was, in time, able to attend certain schools. Attending a school for the deaf in New York, Helen learned German, and attending a school for the blind in New England, she learned Greek and Latin.

Hence, Helen was able to enter one of the nation's finest colleges, Radcliffe, and still accompanied by Anne (who "spelled" the professors' lectures on Helen's palm using a sort of agreed-on shorthand), became the first blind-deaf-dumb person—man or woman—ever to graduate from a college.

Anne's teaching was phenomenal, but she could never have accomplished so much if Helen had not had an indomitable spirit, a rapier-sharp mind, an avid hunger for knowledge, and an amazingly retentive memory.

After she graduated from Radcliffe (cum laude, one should add), Helen spent the rest of her life trying to help other handicapped people by writing books and by lecturing.

Among her books was one that she wrote about Anne. She lectured not only throughout the United States but she went to Europe, South and Central America, and even to the Far East. Everywhere she brought hope—and, yes, happiness to thousands. She herself was a happy person. She said, "I thank God for my handicaps for through them, I have found myself and my God." But perhaps her message is best condensed in these words of hers, "Dark as my path may seem to others, I carry a magic light, Faith. The spiritual searchlight illumines the way. I walk unafraid toward (the place) . . . where life and death are one in the presence of the Lord." A motion picture, *Deliverance,* is based on her autobiography, *The Story of My Life.*

Helen and Anne would be ideal people to end with, except that so many more long liberated ladies (even if by comparison they seem lesser souls) deserve at least mention. So to continue in an up and down pattern from personality to personality, there are the flamboyant sisters Victoria Claflin Woodhull and Tennessee Celeste Claflin. They were not admirable characters like Anne and Helen, but they were certainly colorful. They seemed sensational business-women when they opened brokerage offices in 1869 in New York. Their firm, Woodhull, Claflin and Company, showed a net profit of $750,000 for the first six weeks of business. A then-popular cartoonist drew the sisters in a chariot, pulled by two bulls and two bears with faces of leading financiers of the day.

Later, the National Woman's Suffrage Association nominated Victoria as a presidential candidate at the May 1882 convention. It was a mere symbolic gesture, for (unreasonably and unfairly, be it admitted) women then had no vote in the United States. Still, from the country's beginnings, many women were heard from. In the mid-seventeenth century, Margaret Brent, niece of Lord Calvert, demanded "a place and a voyce" in the Maryland colonial Assembly. Though she was ejected, she later had her chance. When Calvert died, she, the executrix of his will, became in his stead acting governor. Then she not only attended the Assembly, she presided over it—briefly until the righteous males decided that she "set a bad example for ye wives of ye colony".

Even without the vote, some U.S. women had political clout. Mary Elizabeth Lease, whom contemporaries called variously "Lady Orator of the West" and "Kansas Cyclone", in 1890 made 160 speeches in Kansas for the Populist Party, and as a result, the Populists captured the Kansas House of Representatives, electing 91 of 125 members. Supporters proposed her name for the U.S. Senate. Nothing came of that. The first U.S. woman politico to go to Washington was Jeannette Rankin, Republican representative from Montana, in 1917.

A few years later in another part of the world another different sort of liberated lady was making a different sort of history. She was the missionary Edel Quinn, who, because of her organizational ability (but despite her poor health), was appointed in 1936 Legion of Mary Envoy and given the commission to leave her native Ireland and to establish the Legion of Mary in Africa. She traveled all through the east and the central portions of that vast continent, going to many out-of-the-way places. Her means of transportation was a rickety jalopy of uncertain age that was prone to break down, or get stuck in mud, or blow a tire. Nor were Edel's "accommodations" luxury hotels. Discomfort, if not hardship, was her daily bread, but she pursued her work until her death in her late 1930s. (Since she was frail, she expected to die young in any event, so she chose to use what years she had for God.) The Diocesan Process, the first step toward her beatification, has been set in motion by the Archbishop of Nairobi.

Now, a mention of Edith Cavell, the English nurse who was shot by a German firing squad for helping Allied prisoners escape during World War I: "Greater love no man hath . . ."

After these exemplars of heroism, again it is almost a "down" in the pattern to turn to less exalted people, even though they are still exalted when compared to the average. There are, for instance, many liberated ladies eminent in arts and letters. A jumble of names springs to mind. There is the beloved writer of children's books Louisa M. Alcott; the Nobel Prize–winning Danish-born novelist Sigrid Undset, who portrayed such realistic fictional characters against the backdrop of medieval Norway; the Brontë sisters, with their haunting novels; Jane Austen, with her extremely authentic ones; Margaret Mitchell, of *Gone with the Wind* fame; and Harriet Beecher Stowe. Each is so very different, one from the other, but each is a noted long liberated lady in her own way. The last named, Mrs. Stowe, had tremendous impact with her book *Uncle Tom's Cabin*. Regardless of one's opinion of the book, it was indisputably influential; it was a catalyst of the U.S. Civil War. President Lincoln himself spoke of "the little woman who made this big war".

No mention yet of the long liberated lady writers who are poets. Among them are Edna St. Vincent Millay, Emily Dickinson, and Elizabeth Barrett Browning. Certainly, to be a poet is to be inspired with unearthly fire, for as Francis Thompson said, "the function of poetry is to see and restore the Divine idea of things."

Another jumble of names, which is also woefully incomplete, includes artists Mary Cassatt, Rosa Bonheur, and Georgia O'Keeffe; ace photographer Margaret Bourke-

White; singers Ernestine Schumann-Heink, Dame Nellie Melba, Marian Anderson, Jenny Lind, Helena Modjeska, Lily Pons, and Rosa Ponselle; and actresses Sarah Bernhardt, Eleonora Duse, Ethel Barrymore, and . . . oh, many more deserve a word. But it is necessary to stop somewhere! Enough is enough!

THE SECRET FORMULA

If women of the past were so oppressed and suppressed—
and, as pointed out in the first chapter, they did lack some
freedoms—how did the women presented here achieve
liberation and success? Surely feminists would hotly deny
that the few advantages mentioned in the first chapter could
offset the disadvantages that they aver all women of the past
were burdened with. So what was the formula that enabled
these particular women of the past to be such winners? Is
there some sort of mysterious and esoteric formula?

Actually, the formula of our fabulous foremothers, the
long liberated ladies, was the same formula that most really
successful, liberated women of today still use, though they
may not articulate it or may not realize consciously that they
do use it.

Today, for instance, there is world-famous Mother Teresa.
When in 1948 she started out to bring a ray of light into
the dark, filthy streets of Calcutta's slums, when she began
washing vermin-covered bodies and bandaging suppurating
sores, she was not—emphatically she was *not*—heeding
feminists' directives and trying to achieve self-actualization
or striving to garner press clippings and success. She was
not seeking fortune or personal satisfaction; she was only
trying, because she loves God, to help his "least brethren".
However, for her today, honor is piled on honor, including
the prestigious honor of the Nobel Prize. She travels the
world, and everywhere she is received by dignitaries with
honor that verges on reverence.

Parenthetically, a word to those who complain (occasionally with justification) of sexism in the Church: *Nota bene* that it was the Church that gave and gives Mother Teresa backing. Without the Church behind her, she could never have done nor continue to do half the good that is routine with her.

For a second example, there is Phyllis Schlafly. She never sought political clout for its own sake. She never set out to glorify self. She believed and believes strongly in the rightness and the wisdom of certain ideas and principles, and she set out to work for their implementation. George Gilder (in his book *Men and Marriage*) called her "one of the supreme political leaders ever to emerge in America". Whether one agrees with her or not, one has to acknowledge her great feat: it was she who stopped passage of the Equal Rights Amendment to the Constitution after thirty-five state legislatures (that is just three short of those necessary for passage) had voted "Aye", and after about 90 percent of both houses of Congress had backed it. She went over their heads to the people and explained in clear, unequivocal language that the ERA would mean that husbands would no longer be legally bound to support their wives, that the government would be bound to subsidize abortions, that women would not be exempt from combat duty, that the federal government in enforcing the ERA would gain additional power, and so on.

Her opponents desperately tried to defeat her but with no success. Their failure was due at least in part because they never understood the dedication to a belief that is so much stronger than self-seeking. By now, Mrs. Schlafly has received more awards and kudos than she can remember, including, incidentally, the honor of ranking next in line after Mother Teresa in a national poll of most admired women.

For a third example, there is Ethel Waters, the black vocalist and actress who, although she is dead, does not belong with the long liberated ladies; rather she is a present-day liberated lady because many of us remember her and her story almost as well as we remember the stories of the still-living Mother Teresa and Phyllis Schlafly. Ethel had a miserable childhood. Her mother, while a teenager, was raped and conceived Ethel. The child, despite sordid and poverty-stricken surroundings, grew up not thinking of rights, "feminine rights" or any other kind, but with the desire to use the talents that her "precious Jesus" (as she called the Lord) had given her, to make life brighter for herself and for everyone who ever had a heartache, white and black, rich and poor, young and old. She accomplished her desideratum. She reached out—enraptured, inspired, gladdened—and uplifted millions by her singing; then she moved them to tears or laughter by her honest and authentic portrayal of character on the legitimate stage. The result was that she was greatly honored wherever she went. The mighty of the land kowtowed to her, and she made a small fortune.

Where is the unifying thread? What is the common denominator of all the women mentioned in this book from chapter 1 onward, the long liberated ladies and the few women mentioned from the present day?

Well, the three extremely diverse moderns just mentioned, as well as all the long liberated ladies, had the same basic formula. None of them huddled within the cramped, narrow cocoon of her own ego. Each stretched out beyond self, striving to serve a cause or a belief or an ideal or a nation or her fellowman or science and, in the last analysis, consciously or unconsciously, God.

Oliver Wendell Holmes once gave expression to the

formula. He said, "Fame usually comes to those who are thinking of something else."

To concentrate on self, as the feminists do, is to limit one's range and to inhibit one's growth and hence one's value. Albert Einstein said, "The true value of a human being is determined primarily by the measure and the sense in which he has attained liberation from self." Occasionally too, self-concentration means avoiding, through pride, the hard, the menial, the steady, the boringly repetitious, or the unappreciated work that may be necessary for a firm foundation on which to build success.

The lives of these long liberated ladies show clearly that by far the quickest and most direct route to being less than self-absorbed is to be God absorbed and deeply religious, although a few women did manage to avoid self-absorption without being outwardly religious. Marie Curie had no particular formal religion, although she was baptized a Catholic. Nonetheless, she did not work for selfish reasons; she avoided notoriety whenever she could, and she refused to make large sums of money by patenting her discoveries. She worked for science because she believed it could bring incalculable benefits to her fellowman, so really she was working for her fellowman. But since anyone who helps his "least brethren" helps Christ, she was unknowingly serving God.

Then Florence Nightingale, though a religious person, was not one who ran to church constantly. But religious or not, she worked for her fellowman too. Moreover, she was downright self-effacing because she hated publicity and she honestly did not care who got the credit for an accomplishment as long as the work was done. In her effort to shun the spotlight, she deliberately hid behind politicians in getting legislation passed. In the long run, though, it was she who was respected and honored, while the men who introduced the legislation at her urging are forgotten.

Then there was no mention of religion of any kind in a newspaper write-up about a woman who resolved to work for America. Brynhild Haugland wanted to serve America, which had opened its doors to her immigrant Norwegian parents, so she entered politics to work for good government. Born in 1905, she began, when she was past eighty, her twenty-fourth term and her forty-seventh year in the North Dakota House of Representatives. A newspaper reporter, writing of her reelection in 1985, spoke of her "success" and said, "She has held her seat longer than any other female state legislator in the republic."

So there is the paradox: selflessness as long as it is genuine and completely sincere, added to a desire to serve God and man, often leads inadvertently to advantage to self and to success.

And here is another paradox (or maybe it is part of the selflessness): usually, the successful person, while acknowledging her talents, recognizes that they are not exactly hers, or at least that she did not create them; they were God given. She has certain talents in the same way that she has blue eyes or brown eyes, so her part is only to work diligently as a good steward to develop whatever has been handed her.

The brilliant writer Flannery O'Connor, who died so young, understood this. This long liberated lady once wrote, "The writer . . . will feel that whatever his gift is, it comes from God." Ethel Waters understood that too about her vocal and acting abilities.

The person who recognizes the divine Source feels the confidence of immense wealth behind her. When a person thinks she is independent of God, she has only herself to count on; to be dependent on God is to draw on infinite strength and wisdom.

In the instances where self second, service first does not work in the sense of bringing showy success with press clippings and applause (and be it admitted not all feminists, even the noisiest, aim for that), it still brings the "fulfill- ment" that all feminists very rightly do aim for.

Now, if all that we have been saying is true, then a devoted mother who, whenever it is necessary for the welfare of her children, submerges her own wants could be more fulfilled and more successful than most of the women who have attained the limelight that is so often considered the mark of "success".

And truly great success can be hers, though it is hidden. Cardinal Mindszenty called motherhood the most important job on earth, implying that the most important person was the person who performed that job. One tends to agree with him. The writer of this book once wrote elsewhere, "The philosophers who write thick volumes, the engineers who build vaulting bridges, the industrialists who manage international conglomerates—these people by comparison to a mother have insignificant jobs, because even if their success is remembered generation after generation in the spiraling of time, they are limited by time. On the other hand, a mother who rears even one child for his ultimate destiny works not for time but for timelessness, and her efforts will be remembered through the long stretches of eternity."

But actually, in the final analysis, as no doubt Cardinal Mindszenty would agree, the person with the most important job is the person who, regardless of her job on the mundane level, manages to make herself a saint on the spiritual level.

Yes, the saint in any state of life and in any mundane job whatsoever is obviously the most fulfilled and most successful of all women—or men. Whether she ever attains the limelight of earth is irrelevant subjectively as well as objectively, for her faith assures her that she will shine in the immeasurably brighter light of heaven. She is seeking, not her own will but God's will, and if he wills the limelight of earth for her, she will surely attain it. If not, she can be equally fulfilled in her dark little corner, rejoicing that his will is done. Jesus told the mystic Josepha Menendez, who in her lifetime was utterly and completely unknown, "I take delight in your littleness." Consequently, so did she!

So at last, here is the infallible rule to go by. It is an old, old one. Christ taught it when he said, "Seek ye first the kingdom of God and his justice, and all things else will be added unto you."